LEARNING BEYOND THE CLASSROOM

Producing COMPETITIVE Business Results

Executive Learning Exchange
A Collection Prepared by
Dirk Tussing

C/3 PREFACE &O

This book was a collaborative project to create a relevant and actionable collection of meaningful lessons learned, directly authored by learning and talent development thought leaders.

May these pearls of wisdom benefit those attending the 13th Annual 2014 Chicagoland Learning Leaders Conference, held at Allstate Insurance Company in Northbrook, IL, USA.

All proceeds from the sale of this book will benefit RightStart4Kids (www.RightStart4Kids.org), a 501(c)(3) tax-exempt non-profit organization that focuses on initiatives to help children across the globe start life out right from the womb.

Only when children's bodies grow healthy
do we have the opportunity to grow their minds.

Dirk Tussing

Executive Learning
EXCHANGE
Leading Learning Innovations of the Future

✂ CONTENTS ✍

Foreword   ix

STRATEGY   1

1. Lisa Perez   3
   Aligning HR Strategy with the Business: From Vision to
   Execution

2. Aaron Olson & B.K. Simerson   5
   Building Strategic Thinking for New Leaders

3. Pamela S. Puryear   7
   Culture and Strategy Should Meet for Breakfast

4. Jeff Carpenter & Jenny Massoni   9
   A Few Key Questions to Ask before You "LEAP" into
   Social Learning

5. Ann Wyatt   11
   Infusing a Culture of Health

6. Marty Rosenheck   13
   Nano-Coaching: The Key to On-the-Job Learning That
   Gets Results

7. Andy Maus & Carmela Richeson   15
   Strength and Cross-Training

OPERATIONS   17

8. Terrence C. Hackett   19
   Attention Please: The On Demand Revolution Has
   Arrived!

9.   Michelle Burke   21
     Building an Operations Pipeline through Action Learning

10. John R. Mattox, II & Heather Muir   23
     **Can Communications Training Really Improve
     Operations?**

11. Eric Bruner   25
     **Don't Fight Nature: Use Reinforcement to Drive
     Adoption**

12. Judy Whitcomb   27
     Never Lose Sight: Your Internal Customers Have Choices

13. Lacey Jennings   29
     **Self-Directed Learning Increases Motivation and
     Engagement**

14. Joan Cooney   31
     Transforming a Sales Training Team

     PEOPLE   33

15. Tom Griffin   35
     **The "BOTH/AND" Leader: Balancing Essence and
     Form**

16. Laci Loew   37
     **Co-Creation Labs: An Innovative Approach to Leadership
     Development**

17. Cory Bouck   39
     Give Away Your Power to Get More Done!

18. Lisa Schumacher & Gabi Zolla   41
     Know What Your Employees Know

19. DeBorah Lenchard   43
     Put the Spotlight on Informal Learning!

20. Paulo Goelzer 45
    Retail Strategy and People Development

21. Linh Lawler 47
    Stealth Development: Learning Under the Radar

    MEASUREMENT 49

22. Wendy Fencl 51
    Creating an Analytics Strategy: Keep It Sweet and Simple

23. Babak Salimi 53
    Creating Talent Management Metrics

24. A.D. Detrick 55
    Engagement Metrics: Using Behaviors to Optimize Results

25. Kent Barnett 57
    Managing Talent with Net Promoter Score

26. Bill Terpstra 59
    Measurement: One Size Does Not Fit All

27. Alex Draper & Tom Morehead 61
    Using Metrics to Sustain Culture and Leadership in a Period of Rapid Growth

28. Laura Coons & Tiffany Yates 63
    Using RCI: How Fast Can They Learn?

    About Our Thought Leaders 65

    Acknowledgments 103

❧ FOREWORD ❧

The topics of leadership, learning, career management, and analytics are all critically important to business and HR leaders around the world today. One of the biggest issues companies now face is their ability to engage, develop, and lead a new generation of employees—people who are increasingly mobile, more diverse, and demanding. Only by staying current on new ideas, technologies, and global trends can we make sure we are always providing the leading performance-driven solutions to our organizations. This book collects a wonderful combination of solutions and examples we can all use to learn and improve our own strategies.

Josh Bersin
Principal and Founder
Bersin by Deloitte, Deloitte Consulting LLP

Executive Learning
EXCHANGE
Leading Learning Innovations of the Future

STRATEGY

ALIGNING HR STRATEGY WITH THE BUSINESS: FROM VISION TO EXECUTION

Contributed by Lisa Perez, Kohl's Corporation

As resources continue to be strained and the cliché of doing more with less becomes a part of everyday life, we often struggle with this question: What is more important—strategy or execution? Doing both exceedingly well is a must in our current environment. Producing competitive business results demands a cohesive tie between business needs and the Human Resources (HR) focus. Excellent business leaders understand this concept; the tough part is how to go about it. Five key elements make the difference in linking an HR strategy to the business.

The first and most important element is a business leader relationship that builds on trust. The dialogue necessary to translate the company's strategy happens only when HR leaders and business leaders trust one another's expertise, intentions, and track record for honoring commitments and shared experiences. Encouraging business leaders to articulate how their departments will contribute to broader imperatives and how HR can support them is the foundation for producing competitive business results. Correct interpretation of needs and initiative design happen when the right questions are asked and there is enough trust to engage business leaders in open dialogue about solutions that are business centric.

Once there is clear understanding of the initiatives HR can support, establishing a solid plan for execution is critical. Don't hesitate to get outside help and expertise, especially when attempting something for the first time or a complicated initiative. Operating as a solo expert doesn't

3

always yield results. Using outside partners invites innovation into how initiatives are designed and delivered. Count on the plan changing. Leave room for the unknown, and changes in external and internal variables.

Invest time in leveraging relationships by ensuring leadership's alignment with key stakeholders. A great way to validate the HR Strategy co-created with business leaders is to share the plan and begin conversations about measuring success. Who is on board becomes apparent quickly once business leaders are asked to agree to specific success criteria. Business-centric success criteria, or key performance indicators (KPIs), that are defined with the business are far less likely to be challenged or dismissed once the strategy is delivered.

Regularly monitor the execution of the HR Strategy and revise as needed, leveraging the contingency built for course correction. Keep the end goal—producing competitive business results—in focus along the way.

Finally, as major initiatives that make up the strategy are accomplished, measure the results. Since clear agreement was gained as part of the strategic planning and execution process, the results will be credited to the effort and contributions used to implement the business-driven HR Strategy.

TAKEAWAYS

❖ Relationships built on trust are the foundation for creating an HR Strategy that produces competitive business results.

❖ Create a solid plan for executing the HR Strategy, including contingency, outside expertise, and leadership alignment.

❖ Co-create business-centric success measures, periodically review the measures, adjust plans as needed, and share successes.

BUILDING STRATEGIC THINKING FOR NEW LEADERS

Contributed by Aaron Olson & B.K. Simerson, Aon

Learning has become a well-established plank in the modern enterprise. The typical CEO can speak about the importance of "being a learning organization." This recognition serves as a solid platform for new leaders to stand upon in contributing to their organization's vision and mission.

An environment supportive of learning does not guarantee success; new leaders risk squandering the opportunity if they don't bring relevant insights and solutions to the table. We call this strategic thinking, and we've spent the last five years teaching it to graduate students at Northwestern University. We consider strategic thinking to be one of several focus areas in the broader topic of strategy, along with strategy formulation, strategic planning, and strategic management.

One area where new leaders can often quickly contribute is around the topic of human capital management—the way that the organization attracts, manages, and retains its workforce. When applied to the topic, strategic thinking involves these five specific and related activities: recognizing the business value proposition and strategic intent, goal, or objective; identifying the competitive factors at play in achieving that objective; articulating the talent management tactics required to enable that strategy; determining the skill and knowledge issues essential to those tactics; and proposing an integrated solution to address those skill and knowledge issues.

For example, a company that seeks to offer services with differentiated value—and thus command a premium price—depends on employees who can support that value proposition. The organization will need to attract, develop, and retain talent accordingly, and more effectively than its competitors. A learning solution will be more compelling to sponsors and more aligned to the business if it clearly supports that customer value proposition, and complements other elements of how employees are hired and rewarded.

A solid understanding of business alignment helps strengthen the influence of the new leader. It also enhances the success rate of recommended solutions, particularly by mitigating risks of misalignment farther up the "strategic ladder."

New leaders interested in enhancing their strategic-thinking skills can do three things: Read up by selecting an article or book about the basics of strategic management; learn as much as you can about your business by speaking to (and learning from) leaders throughout your organization; and explore opportunities to participate in business discussions without limiting yourself to your specific role or area of expertise. For example, add value during a meeting by pointing out considerations and implications of issues being discussed, even when your functional area's topics fall later in the agenda.

TAKEAWAYS

❖ To add value, articulate the link between your organization's business strategy and its talent acquisition, management, and retention.

❖ Be able to describe how any proposed solution links to a business goal and to other aspects of attracting, retaining, or rewarding the target audience.

❖ To lead strategically, you must understand your business: Seek out ways to get involved and learn, extending beyond your specific role or area of expertise.

CULTURE AND STRATEGY SHOULD MEET FOR BREAKFAST

Contributed by Pamela S. Puryear, Ph.D., Hospira

"Culture eats strategy for breakfast" is attributed to Peter Drucker, an influential thinker on modern management theory and practice. But is it true?

If strategy is most broadly defined as "where we are going" and "how we are going to get there," it provides vision and a plan. Strategy does not speak to how to engage people to execute against that plan. That happens, in part, by helping them understand "how we do things around here," or the culture. Great leaders, enabled by great learning organizations, create culture that drives business performance.

So, does culture eat strategy for breakfast? Strategy cannot be implemented without regard to culture, and culture without strategy is equally doomed. It is rather a paradox where both culture and strategy are required for success. Success is found when the two are aligned.

At Hospira, the arrival of a new CEO created an opportunity to examine culture and to reinforce alignment between culture and strategy. The then-new CEO started using language to describe what he was looking for—behaviors he thought would drive success. The language he used was translated into eight cultural anchors ... or "how we do things around here." The anchors include being customer centric, accountable, and responsible, and focusing on the "main thing."

As the cultural transformation was launched, it was aligned with the organization's strategic priorities, creating to a multi-faceted approach.

A *communications plan* was launched, incorporating the eight cultural anchors that became the centerpiece. *Integration* of the cultural anchors into multiple programs and processes was initiated so that culture is part of everyday conversation. The integration of the cultural anchors into Hospira's 2013 Cascade Strategy Playbook was key to aligning culture and strategy. A *top-down leadership* approach was employed to engage leaders in transforming culture. The centerpiece of this effort was a learning program designed to develop the mindset, behaviors, and necessary leadership skills to drive culture change through their alignment, role-modeling, and expectation-setting throughout the enterprise. *Grassroots engagement* was critical to embed culture at every level. *Reward and recognition* programs to reinforce the desired behaviors were launched and modified to highlight accomplishments supporting culture transformation.

So, perhaps rather than eating strategy for breakfast, culture should meet strategy for breakfast, and together they can align to drive superior business performance.

TAKEAWAYS

- ❖ A desired culture should be defined based upon strategy and aligned with desired business outcomes.

- ❖ Culture should be created and led from within, because a more organic approach will minimize rejection by the organization.

- ❖ For cultural change to stick, it must be communicated, integrated, role-modeled by leaders, embraced by employees, and rewarded.

A FEW KEY QUESTIONS TO ASK
BEFORE YOU "LEAP" INTO SOCIAL LEARNING

Contributed by Jeff Carpenter, Caveo Learning &
Jenny Massoni, Astellas Pharma Global Development Inc.

Social tools are changing how organizations deliver learning solutions by providing users with new ways to interface with training materials and collaborate with others. For this reason, "social" is the new buzzword in learning.

The good news is that social learning gives learning professionals a new set of tools to meet their objectives. The bad news is that many L&D organizations are under pressure to add social learning quickly, without first assessing how the new tools will amplify performance improvements.

Asking a few key questions prior to implementing social learning platforms will help ensure they are delivering recognizable business benefit.

What is the Expected Future State of Your Organization?

Which key initiatives will drive this future state? What skills are most needed to ensure these initiatives are successful? How can users share information to increase their ability to develop and hone these skills?

How Might Social Learning Facilitate the Future State?

What are the communication gaps in the current learning solutions? Are there ways to speed the communication, decrease seat time without lessening performance improvements, make it easier for learners to access or share best practices, and/or provide a better method for the training teams to monitor and guide the learning? Can social learning tools close these identified gaps or meet the other criteria?

What Are the Organizational and Departmental Key Performance Indicators (KPIs)?

How do your internal stakeholders measure and report their successes? Can you connect the dots between the benefits of social learning platforms and their KPIs? Can you report the increased "lift" without resorting to metrics unique to social learning (e.g., followers, shares, and reach)?

Is Social Learning Doing What Was Expected?

How will you track and measure the impact social learning has on the training solution(s)? Will you be able to show (again in KPIs used by other departments) that social learning is providing value and delivering continuous improvement?

As with many processes, these questions represent a cycle that should be revisited based on the KPIs outlined in the planning process.

More social learning tools will become available every year. Avoid the urge to implement individual tools in isolation, and rather ask the questions above to ensure your business will benefit in a recognizable, reportable, and measurable way.

TAKEAWAYS

❖ Before adding any social learning technology, ensure it fits into the overall learning and performance support strategy by determining the specific gaps it fills and performance benefits it delivers.

❖ Use the same KPIs that the greater business and the other departments do when assessing and reporting the value of social learning tools.

❖ When adding social learning to in-progress initiatives, create dashboards that show the performance levels both *before* and *after* the social platform was introduced, as well as ongoing continuous improvement.

INFUSING A CULTURE OF HEALTH
Contributed by Ann Wyatt, HealthFitness

The most common chronic health conditions cause U.S. employees to miss an average of ten work days per year, and about half of adult Americans have one or more chronic health conditions, according to the Centers for Disease Control and Prevention. Considering these statistics, how do employers maintain an engaged, productive workforce? Employers look to onsite wellness programs, but not just any program is effective.

Recent surveys indicate that 60% to 83% of employers offer some form of wellness program. These programs range from those that simply offer an online wellness platform with self-directed tools, to a more comprehensive program that includes screenings, health assessments, coaching, and an onsite team of professionals dedicated to improving employee health. Not all programs are created equal.

An effective wellness program requires a strategic plan, targeted programs, and dedicated resources to build and sustain a culture of health. Successful programs are differentiated by engaged senior leaders who fund the programs, communicate its value, and reward successes.

For example, Brunswick Corporation, leading manufacturer of recreational and lifestyle brands, dedicated a portion of its annual senior leadership meeting to addressing the importance of its wellness initiative to the bottom line and employee well-being. Plus, as part of that initiative, Brunswick implemented a 10-week online challenge called "Get Fit on Route 66," where employees were encouraged to make physical activity a daily habit.

Employees competed for prizes individually and as part of their location. Senior leaders at each of the company's 40+ locations posted weekly updates of average minutes logged per employee. After the challenge concluded, the Vice President of Human Resources for the Boat Group traveled to the location with the strongest participation and presented the award in person.

The gold standard for establishing and implementing a wellness program starts at the top, engages employees, and makes it easy for everyone to participate. This includes making health part of your core business strategy by expressing your company's passion and direction for health and productivity in its mission, vision, or goal statements.

It involves developing a strategic approach to wellness that includes input from C-suite leadership, managers, and eligible employees. And it requires line leaders to be front and center in communications about the wellness program, and first in line for wellness activities.

To make health the easy choice, offer tools such as health assessments and screenings to keep employees abreast of their current health status. Provide interventions for health improvement and condition management.

When company leaders take the necessary steps for the right type of wellness program, they drive their human capital goal of an engaged, productive workforce.

TAKEAWAYS

- ❖ A strategic approach to employee health is more effective than simply offering a wellness program.

- ❖ Managers are the lynchpin that make or break a culture of health in the workplace.

- ❖ Employees listen to words but trust behavior exhibited by management. Managers must participate and show their support of employee health initiatives.

NANO-COACHING: THE KEY TO ON-THE-JOB LEARNING THAT GETS RESULTS

Contributed by Marty Rosenheck, Cognitive Advisors

There is growing recognition that employees develop workplace skills primarily through on-the-job experience. However, the success of on-the-job learning depends on coaching by managers who are short on the time, skills, and knowledge needed to coach effectively. The solution? Nano-coaching.

Elliott Masie, a well-known futurist and expert on workplace learning, defines nano-coaching as "very short burst support." Today's mobile technologies provide exciting opportunities for nano-coaching interactions that are targeted to specific work tasks.

Many organizations have instituted "manager as coach" initiatives, including coaching workshops and information. Despite these efforts, most managers do not provide effective coaching and feedback at the time of need, because they often feel over-burdened and under-prepared. They also question the value of traditional coaching that occurs in long infrequent sessions, are too general, and too removed from the action. Since there is often no tracking or accountability, coaching rarely gets done.

Technology-enabled nano-coaching, on the other hand, occurs in very short and direct interactions. It's targeted to specific work tasks, trackable, asynchronous, and includes performance support for the coaches.

The Water Quality Association (WQA) developed a successful on-the-job learning program using mobile devices to support a nano-coaching workflow. WQA members' sales representatives and technicians who participated in a pilot of the approach were offered a structured on-the-job learning path accessible through mobile devices.

Using their smartphones' sensors (camera, audio and video recorder, and GPS), employees captured evidence of work at each step along their learning path and submitted that evidence to their designated manager-coaches. Managers received an automated email notification that prompted them to review employees' submissions. When they had a few minutes, managers provided short written or recorded audio feedback that was sent back to the employees. The managers were provided with coaching guides, checklists, and success criteria on their smartphones to ensure the coaching and feedback was very targeted, focused, and accurate.

Manager-coaches who participated in this mobile-enabled nano-coaching pilot said that the short interactions on specific work activities actually improved their relationships with their employees and made them more confident in their employees' capabilities. "I love the ability to communicate back and forth with my employees," said a manager who coached new hires during the pilot. "I love being proactively prompted that something is ready for me to review. This system gives me a reason to talk with my people about customers and issues so I can tell if they understand what they're learning. I liked it so much I want to coach more people."

TAKEAWAYS

❖ Effective coaching by managers is critical to the success of on-the-job learning that results in top-notch performance.

❖ Traditional coaching that occurs in long, infrequent, unfocused sessions can be seen as unproductive by managers and is often made a low priority.

❖ Nano-coaching, supported by mobile technology, enables frequent, short, targeted, asynchronous coaching interactions, and makes it easy for managers to support their employees in getting business results.

STRENGTH AND CROSS-TRAINING

Contributed by Andy Maus & Carmela Richeson, Claire's Stores Inc.

Why did the football player take ballet classes? Football players focus and dedicate much of their daily lives to strength training, directly building the skills and endurance to be effective on the field. Flexibility, on the other hand, helps players to avoid tackles, make catches, and reduce the likelihood of injuries to joints such as the knees and shoulders. Ballet relies on flexibility to create graceful movements and intricate footwork. Football players who study ballet receive training that increases their abilities beyond what they would likely achieve using only standard football training drills and exercises.

The football player cross-training in ballet provides a powerful example of how people effectively learn and develop in the workforce. When planning to develop an individual, cross-training—in sometimes seemingly unrelated areas—can benefit overall learning and development. Self-development skill building should also be included in the mix.

So, how can this combination of strength and cross-training be brought to life? The first step is to communicate and provide transparency to the variety of roles and related skills that exist. Publishing "career maps" that outline key roles and related skills in the organization, advertising roles on the organization's career site, and exposing employees to functions in a collaborative learning environment could help to accomplish this. As with the football player and coach, somehow they had to step outside of traditional techniques and discover other ways to improve performance.

The second step is to create an individual development planning strategy and process that complements this combination. The communication, training, and Individual Development Plan process should emphasize the on-the-job learning experience and guide the cross-role or cross-functional learning experiences, leveraging the information communicated above.

The third step is to provide managers and their team members with the individual developing planning tools to plan out in great detail what strength training and cross-training activities can enhance their skills. Mapping these items out helps to draw the linkages between the role of "football player," and the discovery of how learning new skills in "ballet" may propel their success in current and future roles.

The combination of strength and cross-training doesn't suggest that the football player is taking ballet classes to become a ballerina. In fact, the player may never demonstrate extraordinary skill in ballet, but he will become a better overall football player. Similarly, expose your "football players" to learning and practicing new skills in "ballet" through a process and approach that makes those cross-training connections possible.

TAKEAWAYS

- ❖ Blend strength and cross-training. Strength training will build depth of expertise for the employees' current roles. Cross-training will build breadth and accentuate the skills needed to develop for new and future roles.

- ❖ Focus on skill development that is both role based and personal. Understand what an employee needs to develop to maximize all skills as the manager starts to shape developmental experiences on the job.

- ❖ Leverage strengths and further enhance skills through cross-training activities as part of an individual's development plan. It will maximize their learning experience and complement their strengths.

Executive Learning
EXCHANGE
Leading Learning Innovations of the Future

OPERATIONS

.

ATTENTION PLEASE: THE ON DEMAND REVOLUTION HAS ARRIVED!

Contributed by Terrence C. Hackett, Deloitte

The on demand trend has arrived. On-demand learning is a powerful revolution, and now is the time to embrace its power for three reasons: Our world is on demand; work is on demand; and with the onset of technology, anyone can do it.

Our World is On Demand

We live in an on-demand world. Case in point: Every month, 1 billion users across the globe watch over 6 billion hours of videos on YouTube. That's about an hour for each person on the planet. About 40% of those views come from mobile devices. We now expect everything on demand: movies, music, and information of all kinds. We expect this type of access outside of work, so our places of work have no choice but to follow suit.

On Demand Works

Simply put, the model of short, easy-to-access knowledge available anytime, anywhere is brilliant. Studies consistently show that unless we apply what we learn in our training classes, we forget most, if not all, of what we learned. The beauty of on demand is that it's available to us in our moment of need—when we have a question, when we're confused, when we really need an answer. Being able to watch and listen to a short tutorial—more than once if necessary—helps us address whatever issue we have and then move on in our work. We know that no one form of learning is the magic cure—in the classroom or beyond. We need all of them. We need to provide people with as many opportunities to learn as possible.

Anyone Can Do It

Shooting video used to be a time-consuming and expensive endeavor. However, today cameras, screen recorders, and other tools needed to make on-demand lessons are very affordable. True, solid instructional design is still paramount, but with time and a limited budget anyone can make effective learning on demand. Just check out the power of Khan Academy, which includes over 6,000 no-frills mini tutorials that are accessed by millions of students each year worldwide.

The reality is also that people love to share what they know. In his book *Drive*, author Daniel Pink states that sharing knowledge with others gives us purpose and motivates us. In today's technologically advanced world, the opportunity we have to share what we know is unparalleled.

TAKEAWAYS

❖ To keep pace with our on-demand world outside of work, our places of work have no choice but to evolve and follow suit.

❖ Providing learning on key topics available to us 24/7 helps us be more effective in our work and helps support a successful learning strategy for our businesses.

❖ Anyone can create useful support videos, and people enjoy being useful, helping others, and building their expertise.

BUILDING AN OPERATIONS PIPELINE THROUGH ACTION LEARNING

Contributed by Michelle Burke, KeHE Distributors

At a former employer, when the operations team was faced with three open manager positions at one time, they realized that none of the supervisors on the team could be advanced. The supervisors simply hadn't been developed, so they weren't ready for manager positions. This forced the operations team to hire all three positions from outside of the company. Unfortunately, the company had to accept a lengthy learning curve that impacted its ability to meet critical KPIs.

This critical business vulnerability quickly led to a partnership with the talent management team to create a management pipeline. Creating this pipeline would involve defining competencies, measurements, and learning solutions; implementing learning solutions; and measuring impact. Believing strongly in a learner-driven, leadership-supported development model, both leaders and supervisors would be part of creating a program to move forward.

First, leaders defined success profiles detailing the required skills, competencies, and experiences for their supervisors. Each manager then used these profiles to baseline current skills, competencies, and experience levels for each of the incumbents. Next, during a four-hour session, the supervisors were introduced to the profiles and expectations for the program. They were invited to brainstorm specific development activities necessary to close the gap to the next level.

For example, for the "ability to adapt" competency, participants considered approaches to gain experience where they would be forced to be adaptable in the moment. One participant suggested being part of an action learning team working on solving a business problem outside of their direct area of responsibility. Another participant suggested swapping roles with another supervisor twice a week to learn about another part of the business.

Participants left this kick-off session energized to work with their managers to create their personal development plans. These plans included traditional training as well as learning outside of the classroom, employing mentoring, special assignments, or job rotations. Each participant had 90 days to complete their plans. Regular check-ins with managers ensured timely feedback. In addition, a private group was created on an internal social network to allow participants to share their experiences with others.

After 90 days, during a capstone session, each participant was asked to reflect on their learnings, the outcomes of their experiences, and the next steps on their journey toward readiness. Leaders as well as participants then re-assessed the supervisors' competencies. By using the baseline and this subsequent measurement, additional learning solutions were recommended. The team also used this information to further validate our 9-Box talent review process as well as succession planning.

TAKEAWAYS

As you reflect on our organization, keep these three things in mind:

❖ Creating "ready now" successors requires experiential learning that occurs outside the boundaries of a classroom.

❖ Learners who co-create learning plans with managers will take more ownership of completing the plan.

❖ When learners are asked to reflect on what they have learned from their experiences, they connect activity to learning outcomes in a meaningful way.

CAN COMMUNICATIONS TRAINING REALLY IMPROVE OPERATIONS?

Contributed by John R. Mattox, II, KnowledgeAdvisors &
Heather Muir, Mandel Communications

Communication spans all aspects of a business, influencing day-to-day operations in the most basic ways. Is it possible, then, for professionals to measurably improve their performance and productivity—and, thus, the operations of a business—by learning to communicate more effectively? To answer this question, a sound measurement strategy would be needed.

Communications training has been around a long time, and is generally accepted as having powerful impact on day-to-day functions and long-term careers. Anecdotally, great communications training produces results. Stories such as the student who transformed herself from an introverted, sit-behind-the-screen computer programmer to an assured woman, unafraid to take charge of her career, are common. However, where's the hard data?

KnowledgeAdvisors worked with Mandel Communications to do what many consider difficult or impossible: measure the effectiveness of its communications training programs. How did they accomplish this?

They started with the premise that essential delivery and reinforcement tools must be in place in order for communications training to measurably improve learner performance. Also, the training must be delivered in a way that the learner can acquire knowledge and skills. Opportunities to apply newly acquired knowledge and skills must be afforded the learner. Support tools and materials should be available as reference tools and job aids.

Finally, managerial support must be provided to reinforce successful performance and correct unsuccessful performance.

To evaluate the effectiveness of the programs, KnowledgeAdvisors delivered an evaluation to thousands of Mandel's learners, asking them to provide feedback about what they learned, whether they applied the learning, and how much the training had improved their job performance.

The data confirmed the quality and value of Mandel's training, which should reassure L&D purchasing managers that communications training has direct value for organizations. Participants don't just learn. They use what they learn. For example, 96% of respondents indicated they applied training within 6 weeks, leaving only 4% scrap. Scrap is unapplied learning, and for many organizations the scrap rate is 50%. That is, half of all training is wasted. For this communications program, scrap is almost zero, meaning the training is applied and therefore valuable to both the individual and the organization.

Seventy-nine percent of respondents indicated their job performance improved in terms of presentation and conversational skills, with an overall productivity increase of 12%. Sales professionals indicated that training helped them speed up the sales cycle. A project manager indicated he is more productive because he uses a standard email template; it helps his stakeholders reach consensus quicker.

The successful results from this evaluation highlight what many L&D managers have known for years: Communications training works. Some programs will be better than others, but now we know for sure.

TAKEAWAYS

- ❖ It is a misperception that the effectiveness of soft-skills training cannot be measured.

- ❖ Mandel Communications successfully measured the impact of its communications training on individual performance.

- ❖ Evaluation can be used to link training to business outcomes.

DON'T FIGHT NATURE:
USE REINFORCEMENT TO DRIVE ADOPTION
Contributed by Eric Bruner, GP Strategies Corporation

Who was the MVP of the 2014 Super Bowl? Who won the 2010 FIFA World Cup? Chances are you don't remember. Malcolm Smith from the Seattle Seahawks won the MVP award, and Spain won the 2010 World Cup. Interestingly, employees probably spent more time watching and reading about these events than they did in their last corporate learning event! So, how likely is it that learners will adopt the information put forth in our continuous improvement initiatives?

It's commonly known that little is retained from learning interactions, and many may be familiar with the forgetting curve that shows how quickly the human brain allows new learning to fade. Even when learning is business-focused and engaging, the key to both initial learning and subsequent changes in behavior is reinforcement.

Brain retention occurs only if the information is repeatedly recalled, reinforced over time, and built upon constructs already resident in memory. This is exactly why it is so difficult to instill changes in human behavior that are needed to drive business results. Even when the barriers associated with initiative adoption and resistance to change are minimized, the brain simply doesn't remember what to do differently.

Recently, GP Strategies revamped the initial phase of a yearlong project management certification program from a week of intensive classroom activities to a two-day engagement. In-person interaction and exposure to executive leadership has always been a main driver of the weeklong format, but the time away from work responsibilities and the extreme information overload was proving detrimental.

The key to shortening this event was a coach-facilitated, post-training program that served to both reinforce key concepts and allow deeper exposure to content areas that required more detailed coverage. Learners completed weekly micro-learning assignments, and then shared results virtually via social media and webinar formats. Feedback has been highly positive. The prolonged exposure has created both a tighter community and greater comprehension as the reinforcement activities were coordinated with the yearlong certification requirements.

TAKEAWAYS

❖ Regardless of content and mode of intervention, the human brain requires reinforcement to absorb new information.

❖ Micro-learning offers engaging mechanisms to deliver both initial and reinforcement training.

❖ Reinforcement activities should not be random. Rather, they should be aligned with the learning program design, tracked to ensure learner participation, and, most importantly, adapted based on feedback from the learners and business metrics.

NEVER LOSE SIGHT:
YOUR INTERNAL CUSTOMERS HAVE CHOICES
Contributed by Judy Whitcomb, Vi

If your internal customers had $1 million to spend any way they wanted to support their organization for training and development needs, how confident are you that you would win their business? How certain are you that your customers wouldn't spend their money elsewhere? Chances are you spend too much time in your office waddling through a plethora of training projects, initiatives, and course completion reports, and not enough time outside of the classroom understanding your internal customer's needs. As learning leaders, it's critical to never lose sight that they have choices. And, like any other product and services organization, we must constantly demonstrate our value proposition.

Learning leaders must use a combination of clarity of direction (strategy), a robust engine room (people, organization, processes), and the ability to get anywhere faster (productivity and competencies) than their competition. So, how do you get there? By maintaining a competitive advantage. The first step is to understand your internal customer's perception of your department brand. Engage and survey your internal customers frequently. Peter Drucker said it best: "What gets measured gets managed." Consider establishing a learning council, a governance process, and internal service level agreements to remove internal bureaucracy that impacts your team's ability to innovate and change direction quickly for your customers.

You'll hear this from every learning leader, and it's important: Entrench yourself in the business and with your customers. Understand long-term and short-term business objectives, and find out how you can partner with your internal customers to achieve these goals. Learning leaders must also proactively engage in analyzing business data and problems to uncover how the learning organization can provide solutions and support to more effectively drive the business engine.

Be relentless, and don't accept success at face value. Very often, the real need, real solution is buried deep in the data. For instance, if a new leadership development program is intended to drive employee retention and the goal is to reduce attrition by 10%, and attrition is reduced by 25%, should you stop and celebrate? Yes, and no. Celebrate the success, but take the time to review the data and get to the root reasons why attrition improved—not losing sight that there still may be gold to mine. Engage your customers to understand not only the positive business results, but how you got there, and missed opportunities. This will build trust and solidify your competitive advantage.

TAKEAWAYS

❖ To engage business partners, consider establishing a learning council, governance process, and service level agreements.

❖ Learn outside the classroom; entrench yourself in the business. Analyze data and business problems, and proactively identify performance and learning solutions to support your customer's needs.

❖ Know that your real opportunities may lie in the data from successes.

❖ Develop a roadmap for your customer, and develop multiple solutions to address business needs. Remove roadblocks that may put you at a competitive disadvantage.

SELF-DIRECTED LEARNING INCREASES MOTIVATION AND ENGAGEMENT

Contributed by Lacey Jennings, Intrepid Learning

Only 13% of workers worldwide are engaged. In other words, just one in nine employees feel they are emotionally connected to their jobs with the resources and support needed to succeed. This is according to Gallup's unprecedented study of engagement in 120 countries. Why does it matter? Gallup research also shows companies with engaged employees see a 240% increase in business results. How can the levels of employee engagement be increased? The answer may not be as complex or difficult to enact as one might imagine.

"The fullest representations of humanity show people to be curious, vital, and self-motivated. At their best, they are (self-directed) and inspired, striving to learn, extend themselves, master new skills, and apply their talents responsibly," wrote professors Richard Ryan and Edward Deci.

While nurturing personal learning and a sense of progress and growth in employees is not a panacea to all engagement woes, the act of supporting them in their efforts to learn and grow does move the dial in the right direction. So, what exactly does it mean to support employees' efforts to learn and grow?

One approach is self-directed learning, which can take on many forms depending on the client context. The constant, however, is an employee-centered opportunity to explore an area of interest that relates to an organizational need or challenging problem.

For example, to develop leadership skills, a financial services company created an opportunity for employees to collaborate on some innovative solutions to known business challenges. The stakes were increased by having them present their solutions to senior executives. On another engagement, a front-end self-assessment tool provided insight into financial advisors' strengths and knowledge gaps, so they can work through available content to address their needs.

Stretch assignments were recommended for all employees, on a client initiative to improve mid-level leaders' coaching and employee development skills, not just high-potential employees. The intention was to help employees feel a sense of personal progress in order to combat the feeling of stasis that employees express.

Researchers propose employees have innate needs for self-determination, for opportunities to thrive or create the best possible self-image through achievement. Offering opportunities for employees to learn and grow within the workplace is a way to address this personal need for progress while maintaining productivity.

TAKEAWAYS

- ❖ Enlist employees to solve core organizational and business challenges.

- ❖ Use self-assessments as a valuable tool for personal growth and understanding.

- ❖ Talk to employees to find out what they are interested in, and create stretch assignments to promote and encourage progress. Consciously counteract the notion of getting stuck.

TRANSFORMING A SALES TRAINING TEAM
Contributed by Joan Cooney, Combined Insurance

Reducing costs and increasing capabilities are ongoing initiatives across most businesses. Sometimes the efforts are minimal with little organizational impact, and sometimes they are transformational, requiring significant focus and change management. When Combined Insurance decided to change its training resource model from that of a "traveling trainer" to that of a "local trainer," it was indeed a transformational time that required a purposeful plan to avoid disruption to the business.

Imagine releasing 13 highly skilled, seasoned training personnel responsible for training over 3,000 new agents a year, and replacing them with an all-new externally hired training team in less than 12 months, all while not cancelling any offerings. The plan needed to include hiring new talent, developing that talent, and then timing the release of the existing talent to ensure continued and seamless deliveries of new agent training.

Bruce Tuckman's four phases of team dynamics—Forming, Storming, Norming, and Performing—was used for guidance. According to Tuckman, every team evolves through these four phases. In the Forming phase, the team is positive, excited, and open to new responsibilities. In the Storming phase, the team pushes against boundaries and is overwhelmed. Team members develop a stronger team commitment during the Norming phase. And finally, during the Performing phase, the team hits its stride and works diligently with little friction.

This transformation inspired a new vision for our team as a broad and diverse learning organization. Prior to the Forming phase, we developed a trainer job profile; created behavior event interviewing guides; designed teach-back processes; and identified a skill profile including facilitation experience, instructional design, virtual training, and bilingual capabilities.

Team members enjoyed bringing the new trainers on board, getting to know them, and understanding their potential. The Forming phase was progressing so nicely that it was easy to be fooled into believing that the Storming phase would not come. Each new trainer participated in a 10-week development process; attended monthly communication meetings with vision, mission, and core principles setting; and engaged in several team-building activities.

Despite high hopes, 13 converging personality styles and preferences launched the Storming phase. While detailed preparation had provided a strong foundation, additional communication meetings, employee one-on-one meetings, psychometric testing, and weekly lunch-and-learns were needed to successfully persevere through the Storming phase.

We reviewed over 250 resumes, interviewed over 100 candidates and conducted over 30 teach-back sessions. Even though we successfully brought on 13 trainers between February 2013 and January 2014, and rolled off 13 seasoned trainers, our transformation is not yet complete. We are emerging from the Storming phase and are entering the Norming phase, where we see a strong team coming together to meet organizational demands.

TAKEAWAYS

❖ Prepare! Identify the skill sets and competencies for which you want to hire. This focuses your search and hiring.

❖ Don't hurry the selection process. Yes, the pressure of hiring quickly is oppressive, but do not compromise what you are seeking.

❖ The Storming phase WILL come. Believe, embrace it, and create opportunities to solidify your team.

Executive Learning
EXCHANGE
Leading Learning Innovations of the Future

PEOPLE

THE "BOTH/AND" LEADER:
BALANCING ESSENCE AND FORM
Contributed by Tom Griffin, Sears Holdings Corporation

The business world is replete with examples of failures in leadership that led to organizational disgrace or complete downfall. Just consider Enron, Tyco, Arthur Andersen, World Savings, Fannie Mae, WorldCom, HealthSouth, Qwest, Adelphia Communications, Galleon Hedge Funds, and others. A close look at these cases exposes leadership hypocrisy and extreme self-interest. These scandals demonstrate how leaders can fail to balance essence and form.

Success in leadership comes from the ability to effectively balance both essence and form. Balancing essence and form is a "both/and," not an "either/or" proposition for the effective leader. The key distinction is the understanding that both essence and form are important and required for success, but that essence always precedes form.

For the successful leader, balancing essence and form creates positive tension that is attractive, compelling, and inspiring. It is an integrative journey that requires deep self-examination about what it means to lead with excellence. This process of self-examination has a disrupting effect and stimulates an awakening of one's internal essence or essential qualities. It opens up new, transformative possibilities in the development process. The end result is that when essence and form are purposefully integrated, a leader's true legacy begins to form.

Leadership essence is inside-out. It is about being more. It represents the leader's inner internal voice. It is reflected in one's personal philosophy, ideology, purpose, and values. Finding one's essence is an inner search to discover and live out who you truly are. It requires deep and meaningful reflection about our purpose, strengths and weaknesses, what we stand for, and why.

Leadership form is on the outside. It is about doing more. It is the outward expression of how one leads and represents the behavioral side of leadership, which a leader needs to develop committed followers. Leadership form is reflected in one's conduct, actions, and decisions. Outward manifestations (leadership form) of how we lead others flow from inward realizations (leadership essence) of who we are.

When effectively balanced, these interconnected capacities of essence and form provide leaders with a deeper, richer, and more intuitive awareness and appreciation of their leadership journey. Balancing essence and form is ultimately a growth process. It requires a conscious commitment by leaders to lead with their values, connect them with organizational practices, and create a culture that optimizes performance and accountability. By doing so, a leader develops a more inclusive perspective that increases self-awareness, sharpens creative insights, and strengthens the ability to bring out the best in others.

TAKEAWAYS

For leaders, the benefits to balancing *both* essence *and* form are unmistakable. Balance develops the leader's capacity to be more authentic, inspirational, and empathic.

❖ Through authenticity, leaders become more aware of their purpose and personal values.

❖ Through inspiration, leaders develop the capacity to motivate and teach through personal experiences and stories.

❖ Through empathy, leaders more effectively relate to others' stated and unstated emotional needs.

CO-CREATION LABS: AN INNOVATIVE APPROACH TO LEADERSHIP DEVELOPMENT
Contributed by Laci Loew, Brandon Hall Group

The level of complexity in today's business world is unlike any other time in history. Leaders are increasingly challenged to drive business results in tumultuous, uncertain times. The days of command and control leadership are over; collaboration is a requisite success lever. How might a leadership development program build, practice, and drive collaboration in a new and innovative way?

As noted in Brandon Hall Group's February 2014 blog, 80% of organizations still rely on traditional classroom training as their primary approach to leader development. While classroom training can be effective, it alone is not sufficient to build collaborative leadership skills. The best way to *teach* collaboration is through the action of *being* collaborative using a real-world application. How are others doing this? What can be borrowed from other efforts and repurposed for leadership development? Enter the innovative idea of "co-creation."

Co-creation has recently emerged as a proven collaboration approach. It is traditionally focused on enabling and encouraging companies and their customers to co-create products and services through virtual means. How can this be applied to leadership development? In Co-Creation Labs, leaders come together to design their own learning, focus their learning activities on a business challenge, and reflect upon the learning. This type of user-generated learning develops both individual leadership abilities as well as leader networks.

Co-Creation Labs are conducted in a virtual environment at anytime and anyplace, either synchronously or asynchronously. The Labs enable continuous peer networking during which leaders develop and accelerate new ways of thinking and managing complex business challenges.

Co-Creation Labs are effective for bringing leaders from dedicated groups together to build teamwork and relationships. They can be especially powerful in uniting siloed portions of the organization. Due to the Labs' real-world problem solving focus, leaders are more likely to buy in and participate. Further, when senior leadership selects a critical business issue as the focus of the Lab program, invites participants, and expects the presentation of results, the value of Co-Creation Labs goes beyond collaborative learning to driving change and innovation.

Innovating new ways to develop leaders is paramount to remaining competitive in a complex and constantly changing business landscape. In the true spirit of innovation, this is a great time for leadership development functions to partner with innovation teams to explore using innovation techniques and methods for driving the type of leadership development, such as Co-Creation Labs, that matters.

TAKEAWAYS

❖ Collaboration is a key success skill for today's leaders, and new ways of engaging leaders to build this skill are necessary.

❖ Co-Creation Labs build collaboration skills through real-world problem solving when leaders come together in a virtual environment.

❖ Applying innovation rigor to leadership development builds the organizational capability required to sustain business performance in today's volatile, complex, and distributed marketplace.

GIVE AWAY YOUR POWER TO GET MORE DONE!
Contributed by Cory Bouck, Johnsonville Sausage

My career started with nine years as a Naval Flight Officer. Later, after a decade as a businessman, I started thinking about how the military is able to give young men and women so much responsibility and authority, yet maintain extremely high levels of professional behavior and results. I have been repeatedly surprised by how "small" some civilian jobs or roles seem to be, even when held by well-educated and experienced people. I had begun to think that we have become too cautious in the business world, and perhaps more freedom is in order.

When I was 28 years old, my Navy squadron peers and I were regularly given assignments like this: "Fly two airplanes—two crews of 12, and about 10 other maintenance techs—to the other side of the world. Live and work in that foreign city for a month without the benefit of military base support. Fly classified training missions against the host nation's ships and submarines. Kick their butts, but be gracious about it. Be a good ambassador. Work like a team with the U.S. embassy. Keep your planes healthy, and your people fed and safe. Call the squadron if you need any help. But, don't really call." I didn't fully appreciate the magnitude of my responsibilities as a young officer until it was a distant memory because it was the only professional environment I knew.

How does the military do it? It invests highly trained, learning-agile members with huge responsibilities but also the necessary authority that goes with them. Leaders practice their operational and decision-making skills until they have demonstrated mastery under difficult circumstances.

39

Their rules of engagement are specific enough to explain what to do in most cases, but also flexible enough to enable good judgment. Leaders are enculturated with an ethos that demands good behavior and judgment at all times, not just when it is easy. And they are surrounded with human support. That support is the component I was forgetting that I had so much of as a young officer. On my crew of 12, I had the benefit of over a hundred years of experience. Final decisions were mine to make, but I had incredible wisdom available. In today's lean business environment, instead of creatively finding resources to support young leaders, many times the easy way out is to make their jobs "smaller."

What can be done to make peoples' jobs "bigger"? Doing so will grow future leaders who will accept responsibility, and be more likely themselves to view success and failure through the lens of the leadership they provide to others.

TAKEAWAYS

* ❖ The best leaders grow autonomous, empowered teammates, who will be more likely to go on to grow others that way.

* ❖ Giving away power and authority will allow one to accomplish ten times as much through others.

* ❖ View success and failure through The Lens of Leadership you provide to others.

KNOW WHAT YOUR EMPLOYEES KNOW
Contributed by Lisa Schumacher, McDonald's Corporation &
Gabi Zolla, Council for Adult and Experiential Learning

Most jobs of the future will require college credentials; presently, there are numbers of college-age "millennials" without a degree. How do we close this gap to position our leadership pipelines?

The first step is to recognize that many of the younger workforce actually have acquired college-level learning as a result of previous jobs, life experiences, military service, or volunteerism. There are many ways to acquire knowledge and skills. From the classroom, to life, work, and volunteerism, what many people know far exceeds their formally recorded college credits, degrees, and certifications.

The second step is to identify what employees know. Once that question is answered, linking these individuals to educational opportunities where college credits can be received for college-level learning is critical for employers wanting a competitive industry advantage.

McDonald's Corporation is an example of this process in action. Because McDonald's promotes its management from within, it has managers in its workforce without degrees. This is especially important considering that many of McDonald's current millennial workers are its future managers and executives. To encourage those high-performing employees to earn their degree and advance further, the company has experimented with programs such as LearningCounts.org.

Through LearningCounts, the Council for Adult and Experiential Learning

(CAEL) in Chicago works to provide millennials and other adults with opportunities for college credits gained from outside-classroom knowledge. Linked to a network of higher education institutions nationwide, LearningCounts students receive credits for successfully documenting outside-classroom learning, saving time and money in pursuit of a degree.

Success stories include 28-year-old Ryan S. of Colorado, who has saved more than $11,000 of the cost of earning his bachelor's in business management. 32-year-old Jennifer K., who went straight into the workplace after high school, has been able to translate her professional experiences into more than 48 college credits, putting her closer to a degree in human services. 33-year-old David N. of New York City, who previously thought time and money would prevent his return to school, has saved nearly $10,000 of the typical cost of a bachelor's degree in business administration.

A key success factor for employees who can benefit from programs such as LearningCounts is the engagement and support of their managers. Managers must be open to the concept of employees' receiving college credit for college-level knowledge, discussing the employee's history to recognize potential opportunities, linking them with the appropriate educational organization, and building on this foundation.

Millennials are the next entrants to the leadership pipeline, and employers who help these workers continually develop their skill set through all types of educational opportunities will further succeed.

TAKEAWAYS

❖ College degrees are required for leadership positions. Many millennial workers are not currently positioned to obtain these degrees.

❖ Millennials can receive college-level credits for college-level knowledge earned through life experiences, jobs including military service, and volunteerism.

❖ Managers must work with millennials to identify and complete these educational opportunities to maintain a strong leadership pipeline.

PUT THE SPOTLIGHT ON INFORMAL LEARNING!
Contributed by DeBorah Lenchard, Spot Trading

Research indicates that up to 75% of learning takes place informally through community, exploration, and discussion. Further, studies have shown that learning opportunities drive employee retention. What can organizations do to enable and drive the type of informal learning that will retain employees and grow the business?

Spot Trading, a small proprietary trading firm, views learning as a strategic and competitive strength. Spot encourages every employee to take ownership of learning continuously, progress their careers, and share their knowledge and expertise. This approach has improved business processes and productivity, and promoted Spot's business growth. As a result, Spot is proud to have been selected as one of "Chicago's Top Workplaces 2013" by the *Chicago Tribune*.

At Spot, everyone is considered both a learner and teacher. This is communicated as early as recruiting and followed through on-boarding and employment. New employees teach early in their careers, immediately empowering them and increasing their productivity. Project learning partners, a technical book club, impromptu study groups for technical certifications and exams, and open seating enhance collaboration. Everyone has responsibility for building one another's knowledge. As more knowledge has been shared, greater collaboration and less siloed work have improved job satisfaction and streamlined work efforts.

Ideas and insights can be shared just about anywhere at Spot, including on writeable walls, an internal wiki and website, chat and instant messaging channels, new trading application videos, and an engineering blog. Our employees especially enjoy gathering in Spot's onsite library, which has lounge seating, computers, and hundreds of resources. Spot also provides snacks as employees share knowledge at informal Snack & Learns. These spaces, tools, and platforms enable people to share knowledge and ideas, establishing working relationships and interactions that may never have happened otherwise. Informal learning has led to new initiatives, increased idea flow, and improved problem solving.

Line leaders through senior management walk the talk by personally engaging in teaching and learning. They discuss the importance of skill development and participation in learning events, and acknowledge employees in person and through the online platform, "Spotlight on Learning." Leader involvement encourages conversation and establishes a learning culture that maintains Spot's competitiveness.

Informal learning is kept front and center through flyers; broadcasting on the intranet; highlighting achievements online and physically on the writeable walls; celebrating success; and through learning champions who assist in spreading the word. Together, these efforts contribute to Spot's strategic initiatives and growth, and are also critical to shaping the organization's external brand image necessary for recruiting top talent and remaining an employer of choice.

TAKEAWAYS

❖ Tap into the entire employee lifecycle. Set the expectation of employees as learners and teachers during recruiting and on-boarding. Follow by enabling, rewarding, and celebrating efforts.

❖ Provide opportunities to grow and build skills by creating various informal resources (e.g., Snack & Learns, wikis, chat channels, blogs, learning partners, and physical spaces) to share knowledge, including an internal place to network.

❖ Market learning opportunities using virtual platforms, physical spaces, and learning champions.

RETAIL STRATEGY
AND PEOPLE DEVELOPMENT
Contributed by Paulo Goelzer, IGA Coca-Cola Institute

In the retail business, products disappear and stores close because customers are not under any obligation to be loyal. Sustaining a competitive advantage requires a strategy that includes people development—the type that allows the business to distinguish itself through a phenomenal shopping experience. Does your strategy qualify as a winning one?

While many factors enter into designing a winning strategy, efforts fall short when the organization lacks the competencies and capacity to achieve and fulfill its strategy. Employees become frustrated, managers are stressed, senior leaders become puzzled, and customers suffer. Involving key areas of a company in the strategic planning process is key to avoiding this pitfall.

Organizations may not realize the value of human resources in strategic planning and execution. For example, a partnership between line leaders and learning leaders can be pivotal in assessing current skill capabilities, and aligning them to the present and future needs of business. Since retailers are not merely bricks, mortar, shelves, and inventories, they need associates to gain new viewpoints, skills, or knowledge that address the business opportunity at the same rate or faster than the market.

With a common understanding of the strategy and the company objectives in hand, learning leaders and line managers must partner to determine capability shortfalls. The first step is to uncover real world issues by asking questions. Root causes, and not just opinion, are needed to determine one of the most critical questions: Is the capability issue related to a lack of knowledge and skills, or something else? If the issue can be corrected through development, learning from past endeavors with such questions as, "What has been tried before and why didn't it work?" can accelerate improvement.

Many times, issues may appear as development needs on the surface. One of the most common misdiagnoses occurs when lack of motivation is mistaken for a capabilities deficiency. Those unskilled in the learning field can easily misdiagnose, wasting valuable time and money. The learning leader is an essential partner in assessing the appropriateness of proposed learning solutions.

If the reasons for training are related to building competencies to meet new business objectives; improving efficiency; minimizing mistakes; mitigating risks; retaining customers; or improving customer services and shopping experience, it is important that line leaders and learning leaders partner with a common understanding of the strategy. Even the best business plan will not produce a return if it is not backed up by the needed behaviors and performance.

TAKEAWAYS

❖ Involve human resources in strategy development, and partner learning leaders with line leaders for execution.

❖ Uncover the root problems that can addressed through learning solutions.

❖ Ensure learning leaders are skilled and motivated to know when to use and avoid training.

STEALTH DEVELOPMENT: LEARNING UNDER THE RADAR

Contributed by Linh Lawler, Allstate Insurance Company

Imagine this scenario: An executive was adamantly requesting the development of her frontline managers. They needed it. They never had formal leadership training, and some of them have been doing their jobs for as long as 20 years. Unfortunately, this scenario was not limited to frontline managers. Many of her directors didn't have formal leadership training, either. The gaps didn't just lie in the frontline leaders but also their direct supervisors (the directors).

It became quickly apparent that some "stealth development" was required for the directors. What is stealth development? It's providing an engaging opportunity that aligns with the business needs and encourages development for people who do not believe they need it. The opportunity directly supports a business goal or strategy, and yet builds in a developmental component for the participants/audience.

To meet the needs of the frontline managers (and the executive's request), a 9-month leadership development program was designed for incumbent leaders. From there, some stealth development followed. An orientation session was created for the directors to become familiar with what their frontline managers would learn. It was an engaging opportunity to introduce the essential leadership skills, such as coaching and giving feedback, increasing self-awareness in a way that was not directly targeted to the directors.

By positioning the director session as tools and techniques to support their direct reports through the 9-month leadership training, there was immediate buy-in. Components of self-awareness and reflection to the orientation were also included. Some were hesitant—most didn't want to go—but their direct reports were not allowed into the Frontline Manager program unless their direct supervisors attended the required orientation.

In those director sessions, a light bulb came on. They realized that they needed to be integrally involved in what was going on with their leaders' development and the program. Comments such as, "This is great. I need to reinforce this when they get back from training," were heard. The directors were committed to their employees' success.

Something else happened: The directors became excited about their own learning. They were asked to do a self-assessment to better understand what their employees were going to take. Through this process, they realized they had strengths and opportunities to work on as well. They were reenergized about their own development.

Providing the value of this stealth endeavor, the directors requested additional sessions to continue their development. They gave us a list of skills they wanted to learn together. Integrating developmental components into the orientation surfaced the need, and engaged the participants without ever having to declare that need.

TAKEAWAYS

❖ Leadership at all levels can use additional skills or enhancement of current leadership skills.

❖ Leadership programs should include a component that puts the participant's leaders through development as well.

❖ Stealth development gets them in the door, allowing leaders to benefit from a development experience they didn't initially think they needed to have.

Executive Learning
EXCHANGE
Leading Learning Innovations of the Future

MEASUREMENT

CREATING AN ANALYTICS STRATEGY: KEEP IT SWEET AND SIMPLE
Contributed by Wendy Fencl, Heidrick & Struggles

Human capital analytics have gained in popularity over the past few years and become increasingly prevalent. This trend has led to a myriad of activities to capture information that can be quantified, analyzed, promoted, and interpreted. As with the adoption of many other practices, the pendulum of change tends to swing from one end back to the other before reaching a practical middle ground.

Where is this middle ground? As the zenith of this data drive is approached, its intent must monitored. Specifically, the intent should be laser focused on providing information that moves the organization's people strategies forward. Further, the approach should be the old "KISS" adage: Keep it Sweet and Simple. As Coco Chanel advised, sometimes less is more.

In an increasingly complex business world, it's imperative to pare down to the essentials using a few tools and techniques. For example, scorecards are a valuable way to present human analytics information. Since scorecards are widely in use and accepted, this tool can influence action that flows through the main artery of the organization. Scorecards answer foundational questions that inform strategy decisions; clarify what metrics are needed for objectivity and clarity; translate data into requirements; and present the data as information in a logical, compelling manner.

Metrics support the demonstration of an objective's completion. While SMART (Specific, Measurable, Assignable, Realistic, Time-related) is a time-honored litmus test of an objective, strategy can sometimes dictate drawing "outside of the lines." Not every metric is necessarily a good one, and not everything is quantitatively measurable. Most organizations collect data that was important years ago, yet protocols still exist to support them.

Looking at all metric-related outputs critically to assess whether they are valuable, or just a remnant of a previous strategy, is a prudent effort that can refocus the cost of measurements to current requirements. In addition to the "M" for "measurable," it is helpful to consider the outcomes that are a simple yes/no for presentation. The type of qualitative "judgment" measures may be the best determinant of whether or not an objective was met. After all, intelligent leaders are expected to make sound decisions with limited data.

Tell stories. While numbers provide information, they don't provide the meaning that can only come from background, context, and testimonials. Stories influence and persuade because they strike a responsive chord with the audience.

TAKEAWAYS

❖ Parsimony in both process and output will ensure that the audience will focus on the vital information they need and understand your key messages.

❖ Don't abandon sophisticated analytics if needed; rather, seek to adopt a mindset of simplicity as a guiding force in using and presenting learning and development metrics.

❖ Leverage tools such as scorecards, challenging metrics, and stories to convey accomplishments and provide critical information.

CREATING TALENT MANAGEMENT METRICS
Contributed by Babak Salimi, Saba

Over the past few years, organizations have done an unprecedented amount of restructuring, retrenchment, and downsizing. Much of this has been very reactionary, without time to think, plan, or take into consideration the optimal workforce size and structure. Most organizations lack metrics to measure the workforce or measure everything, and don't know which numbers really matter.

Talent management metrics allow organizations to evaluate and analyze talent management practices for recruiting, mobility, performance management, training and development, and turnover and retention. Tracking talent management metrics also enables organizations to hold all levels of management accountable for management practices and quality. It measures the effectiveness of hiring practices, the success of training and development efforts, and cost efficiency.

While many metrics could potentially be included, starting with the following five will provide a balanced dashboard:

New Hire High-Performer Rate – The percentage of new hires rated as high-quality, high-potential, or high-performing employees, depending on each organization's new hire evaluation, and performance management process and standards.

Percent of High Performers – For a particular workforce segment, business unit, or overall organization, this metric measures the percent of the population that is rated as high performing. The best use of this is to hold individual managers accountable for nurturing and developing the organization's most promising talent.

Career Path Ratio – This ratio measures relative upward and lateral mobility. This metric should be calculated by individual manager.

Total Cost of Workforce – While it may be hard to see how cost of workforce relates to talent management, the best managers are actually able to achieve better results while reducing overall workforce costs. Whether it's through more efficient recruiting and hiring methods or using transfers, mobility, or promotions effectively, these managers are able to build—rather than buy—the best talent.

High-Performer Turnover Rate – This metric allows organizations to measure management effectiveness in retaining top talent at the organization. This metric should be calculated on an individual manager basis. For effective talent management at any organization, the focus should always be on identifying, grooming, managing, and retaining top talent.

Organizations that are able to leverage data-driven decision making for the workforce will not only outperform their competitors but also return higher value to shareholders. Additionally, they will be better positioned to meet workforce and business demands for the future.

TAKEAWAYS

❖ Leverage your key metrics to identify potential issues before they become problematic, calculate the financial impact, and formulate a strategy for intervention.

❖ Metrics can help quantify the return on investment (ROI) of workforce decisions, identify employee success profiles, and develop a true talent management strategy at any organization.

❖ HR has a chance to earn a seat at the table, and the credibility to make business and workforce strategy decisions by identifying cost savings opportunities, improving retention of key talent, and increasing workforce productivity and efficiency.

ENGAGEMENT METRICS:
USING BEHAVIORS TO OPTIMIZE RESULTS
Contributed by A.D. Detrick, Intrepid Learning

Employee engagement has historically been a narrow metric, relegated to one or two self-reported questions on an employee satisfaction survey. Now in an age of vast amounts of data, with the ability to track business and performance metrics at an increasingly granular level, these wide, general questions are insufficient. Ensuring our human capital has the knowledge, resources, and motivation to perform effectively has required not only measuring output but also measuring "what" our employees achieve, "how" they achieved it, and "why" they achieved it. Engagement metrics are no longer a personal estimation of contentment, but rather a path to designing our processes and systems to ensure employees are efficiently and effectively getting access to the necessary knowledge and resources.

Unlike most business metrics, engagement is a nuanced series of measurements. As much as we intend to standardize work behaviors to effect outcomes, each employee's performance is unique. But now, more than ever, each employee leaves behind trails of data providing information about how they perform—not just business outcomes, but data on how they *achieved* those outcomes. For example, we can track how often they use specific systems or resources and for how long; how much information they provide; and how much they consume. On their own, these data points may seem meaningless, but if organized and analyzed properly, they provide a clear picture of how our employees are engaged with their jobs.

The best way to measure engagement is to categorize these behavior measurements according to the "Four I's": Involvement, Interaction, Influence, and Intimacy. Monitoring an employee's involvement (how often they engage with the process or system, and for how long) and interaction (how much activity they do when involved) informs our understanding of their behaviors. Influence (how much they advocate on behalf of the system or process by sharing information or contributing to it) and intimacy (how they feel about it—positively or negatively) metrics give a clear picture of their motivations.

Engagement metrics can be a very effective way to identify the best way to ensure optimal performance metrics. Identifying the behaviors that most engage employees can reduce the waste of ineffective or distracting elements. By focusing on behavior as much as outcomes, employees' motivations and pain points are better understood. With a focus on engagement, the vast amounts of data can be transformed into meaningful information that creates a path to help our employees become more engaged with their work, and more effective.

TAKEAWAYS

❖ Engagement metrics are a complement to traditional business metrics. Neither is sufficient in the current Information Age, and neither is irrelevant.

❖ Measure employee engagement by grouping metrics into four categories: Involvement, Interaction, Influence, and Intimacy.

❖ Regularly use engagement metrics to optimize how employees are engaging with the knowledge and resources required to do their jobs. Processes and systems should be designed based on how your employees are most effectively engaged.

MANAGING TALENT
WITH NET PROMOTER SCORE
Contributed by Kent Barnett, KnowledgeAdvisors

Employee engagement has been shown to heavily influence retention and customer satisfaction. Engagement is significantly impacted by six human capital processes, three of which have been shown to be the key drivers of engagement: leadership effectiveness, performance of co-workers, and learning and development experiences. How might human capital processes be measured and used to improve engagement?

Fred Reichheld, author of *The Ultimate Question*, revolutionized the customer satisfaction survey process by bringing the Net Promoter Score (NPS) to prominence. NPS is a single measure of customer satisfaction. Respondents answer the question, "How likely are you to recommend this company to a friend or family member?" and are scored as Detractors, Passives, and Promoters. The percentage of Detractors is subtracted from the percentage of Promoters to produce a Net Promoter Score.

While this approach was designed to measure external customer satisfaction, KnowledgeAdvisors (KA) modified it to measure key talent processes within an organization. KA divides talent into six pillars that cover all human capital processes within an organization: Talent Acquisition, Learning and Development, Capability Management, Leadership Development, Total Rewards, and Performance Management.

In line with the simplicity of the original NPS process, one question was developed for each of the six pillars. The results provided some interesting insights. Through a rigorous analysis process, measures were correlated and entered into a regression equation to determine the key drivers of engagement.

Three drivers rose to the top as carrying the most influence: Leadership effectiveness, Performance of co-workers, and Learning and Development experiences. An organization that has flagging employee engagement should focus on improving these three pillars first as they will have the greatest impact on engagement.

Organizations can use the six pillar measures in many ways. The benchmark values can be used to determine if an organization is over performing or underperforming on any of the pillars. It is important to note, however, that improvement actions will require senior leadership support.

Assuming the model applies to all organizations, efforts to improve leadership effectiveness will improve employee engagement most. Several additional data sets can also be joined with the NPS Talent data to help leaders with decision-making. Joining exit survey results with NPS values can be used to predict which employees may leave. Productivity data can also be linked to determine whether engaged employees are truly productive employees. Likewise, if productivity data are linked with engagement scores, profitability can be predicted. Even recruiting data can be employed to test the hypothesis that a positive hiring experience sets the foundation for an engaged employee.

Talent management metrics can provide substantial value to organizational leaders as they strive to improve employee engagement.

TAKEAWAYS

❖ The NPS approach to external customer satisfaction can be applied to talent to assess the health of talent processes in an organization.

❖ While NPS is a simple talent survey that can quickly determine which talent processes need improvement, it is also a long-term journey requiring a hyper customer-centric measurement and improvement cycle.

❖ Leadership effectiveness is critical to employee engagement.

MEASUREMENT: ONE SIZE DOES NOT FIT ALL
Contributed by Bill Terpstra, Motorola Solutions

When it comes to the measurement of learning programs, some organizations tend to employ a single-pronged strategy, assuming the same metrics apply to all. This type of one-size-fits-all measurement strategy leads to inefficiencies and obscures the effectiveness of the strategic learning solutions that impact business performance. For example, should regulatory training be measured the same way as the training to support a new product launch?

Considering regulatory training, if subject matter awareness is high and the compliance record is in good standing, the organization is essentially in maintenance mode when it comes to training. In this case, a simple Level 1 evaluation, which measures the learners' reaction to the learning experience, is sufficient.

On the other hand, training to support important initiatives such as new product launches; major system or process changes; or evolving organization missions that require new knowledge, skills, and behaviors has a critical impact on the business' success. In those cases, a measurement approach that correlates learning programs to changes in the business' key performance indicators (KPIs) is needed.

Innovative measurement technologies are becoming more accessible and affordable, making a multi-pronged measurement strategy possible. It is now easier to set different metrics for different learning programs and apply relevant measurement tools accordingly. In this way, the toolkit can range from Level 1 surveys to knowledge gain assessments, success case methodology, and comprehensive data analytics tying learning results to business goals. Newer forms of evaluation, such as embedded ratings measures for informal learning assets, and social ratings such as "likes," stars, shares, and comments in online communities can also be used. Other data sources that are not necessarily learning-related but rather measures of customer satisfaction, sales, quality metrics, and average deal size can be used. The "big data"—together with back-end system integration and analytics—can be brought in to enable reporting and dashboards.

For this multi-pronged approach to be successful, we must align closely to the organization's strategy and anticipate the size of performance impact before designing our learning programs. This will guide the selection and design of the most effective measurement strategy and tools. This will allow the learning team and business leaders to stay focused on the business results and employee behaviors that will have the biggest impact on the company.

Learners have different business priorities, needs, and learning styles. Likewise, learning solutions are different in terms of their *mediums* (face-to-face, online, mobile), *formats* (classroom, self-directed online, virtual instructor-led, labs, professional games, peer-to-peer learning, online communities, videos, podcasts, on-demand performance tools) and *lengths* (days or hours of training, bite-size content). Measurement must be varied accordingly.

TAKEAWAYS

❖ Every learning program has varied impact on the business, so the investment in measurement should be commensurate to the impact.

❖ A multi-pronged measurement strategy provides efficiency by matching the right measure to the learning.

❖ Measures should be varied by learning modality.

USING METRICS TO SUSTAIN CULTURE AND LEADERSHIP IN A PERIOD OF RAPID GROWTH

Contributed by Alex Draper & Tom Morehead, ProfitAbility

Shortly after being recognized as one of the "Most Innovative Companies" in 2012 by *Fast Company* magazine, Networked Insights (NI) was faced with an exciting yet daunting challenge to their innovative "start-up culture" and leadership.

In the midst of rapid growth, NI wanted to sustain a strong company culture and build consistent leadership during a period of expansion. The leadership team was determined to ensure that, despite undergoing a tremendous surge in business and employee growth, the company culture and its DNA of award-winning innovation could serve as a major competitive advantage. This competitive advantage was vital given that the entire data marketplace had recently intensified. The new marketplace was typified by huge demand for advanced data analytics, accompanied by requests for much quicker cycle times. The marketing data ecosystem had become a battleground with many larger competing organizations providing "value-added" data analysis.

After strategic planning and design, a comprehensive approach that utilized metrics throughout the entire process was launched. In the data gathering phase, every employee participated in an initial company culture assessment. This survey not only provided many useful baseline metrics, it also helped identify a variety of strategic topics to be discussed. These topics were included in a two-day customized business simulation.

The business simulation workshop was an opportunity for all employees—from the CEO to every new hire—to engage in small-group discussions about the importance of culture, core values, and leadership at all levels across the organization. The baseline survey metrics were shared by leadership in all workshops. Each employee, including the CEO, participated in an intensive business simulation accompanied by metrics on customer satisfaction and financial measurements.

To sustain profitable growth after the initial workshops, senior leadership identified and tracked six organizational performance metrics: Innovation, Sales Growth, Market Share, Customer Satisfaction, Employee Satisfaction and Return on Assets. Leadership also assigned cross-functional teams and used measurement steps to track progress from the initial baseline company survey and the business simulation workshops.

In the following year, the culture survey was delivered to nearly twice as many employees, due to continued growth. The updated survey results and the corresponding six organizational performance metrics highlighted several improvements in the overall culture. "Encouraging Innovation and Risk Taking" remained a top attribute identified by employees.

Metrics can play a powerful role in helping build and sustain company culture. These encouraging results demonstrate just one example of how organizations are using metrics for business success. In order to thrive in a hyper-competitive global marketplace, organizations need to consistently apply metrics related to culture and leadership in the same way they proactively drive business results.

TAKEAWAYS

❖ Apply the same rigor to people and culture metrics as applied to business metrics.

❖ Build trust and engagement by sharing and discussing metrics with all employees.

❖ Focus on metrics to help ensure company core competencies, such as innovation, are sustained even in high growth environments.

USING RCI: HOW FAST CAN THEY LEARN?

Contributed by Laura Coons & Tiffany Yates, Colorado Technical University

Training is impactful only when it is delivered by the time it is required. This article discusses the value and justification for implementing Rapid Continuous Improvement (RCI) to successfully achieve defined learning outcomes within modern transitional organizations. The three components of RCI can be merged within traditional learning models (needs assessing, objective setting, training development, training deployment/delivery, and training evaluation) to exceed training demands within extremely dynamic organizations.

Why is rapidity valuable to learning operations? Rapidity in training ensures operational initiatives can be organizationally meaningful. The luxury of time is nonexistent in changing and energetic environments. Rapid training programs can subsidize the identification of the ideal time to deploy training. Faster learning models can also be delivered on the job for teams that cannot take workers "off the line" to spend time in training. The rapidity approach accelerates training, focusing the trainer and the learning on the practical job highpoints.

Finding the ideal speed is paramount. Training operations must be careful, because too fast can become insignificant and cause white noise. Try not to get stuck in speeding up training that deters the proper pacing to meet the mission of the organizational system. At the same time, be cautious of slothful training that may be discarded due to lack of relevancy, ultimately sacrificing the cost of time, talent, and budget.

Why is continuous improvement valuable to learning operations? Continuous improvement in this context creates repetitive intersections of flexible, adaptable, and fluid deliverables that join all levels of the organizational system. At the macro level, rapid training programs vanish without constant reinforcement. To sustain consistent training improvements, participants are ultimately pulling self-directed learning goals into the system while creating personal meaning in feedback loops of needs. The proper training design carves out the space of intentionality for learning within job function and team dynamic.

Infinite learning outside the classroom is fueled by individual employee learning classification and motivation. Organizational behavior meanings at the micro level of the system can perpetuate personal, sustainable skill advancement. Motivated participants are attracted to continuous improvement training because they value the learning outcomes as positive qualities towards their personal career ambitions.

Personal participant interest can be as subtle as the training program initiatives. Engagement can be fostered through transparency—participant and learning administrators having access to all the same information. Empowering ownership of self-service training narratives drives additional commitment to continuous personal improvement through learning.

TAKEAWAYS

❖ The Rapid Continuous Improvement model ensures a consistent focus on appropriately impactful training.

❖ Training can meet the test of being appropriate and meaningful by leveraging consistent on-the-job interval skill development, empowered by participant self-service and personal motivation.

❖ When an organization values RCI in training operations, the senior leadership can delineate a clear return on investment for skill development through the interconnectors of future aspirations and talent succession planning.

Executive Learning
EXCHANGE
Leading Learning Innovations of the Future

ABOUT OUR
THOUGHT LEADERS

Kent Barnett

Founder, Chairman and CEO

KnowledgeAdvisors

Kent Barnett is the Founder, Chairman and CEO at KnowledgeAdvisors. He has worked with hundreds of companies to implement a broad range of measurement solutions to assess the real impact training has on organizational performance. KnowledgeAdvisors arose from his dissatisfaction with the lack of measurement solutions available to express the relationship between the real impact of training and organizational performance. Prior to starting KnowledgeAdvisors in 1999, Kent was the co-founder and former president of Productivity Point International (PPI). Kent has an MBA from The Kellogg School of Management at Northwestern University. Kent co-authored the book, *Human Capital Analytics: Measuring and Improving Talent Development.*

Twitter:
@KnowledgeAdv

LinkedIn:
www.linkedin.com/pub/kent-barnett/0/948/671

Josh Bersin

Principal and Founder

Bersin by Deloitte, Deloitte Consulting LLP

Josh Bersin founded Bersin & Associates (now Bersin by Deloitte) in 2001 to provide research and advisory services focused on corporate learning. He is responsible for the firm's long-term strategy and market eminence. Josh is a frequent speaker at industry events and has been quoted on talent management topics in key media, including *Harvard Business Review*, *The Wall Street Journal*, *Bloomberg*, on BBC Radio, CBS Radio and National Public Radio. He is a popular blogger for Forbes.com and has been a columnist since 2007 for *Chief Learning Officer* magazine. Josh spent 25 years in product development, product management, marketing, and sales of e-learning and other enterprise technologies at companies, including DigitalThink (now Convergys), Arista Knowledge Systems, Sybase, and IBM. Josh's education includes a B.S. in engineering from Cornell University, an M.S. in Engineering from Stanford University, and an MBA from the Haas School of Business at the University of California, Berkeley.

Twitter:
@Josh_Bersin

LinkedIn:
www.linkedin.com/in/bersin

Cory Bouck

Director of Organizational Development & Learning

Johnsonville Sausage

Cory Bouck is the Director of Organizational Development & Learning at Johnsonville Sausage. He is also an author, keynote speaker, and an expert in building leaders—a reputation he has earned over twenty years of leading in the military, in business, and in politics. He is a graduate of and former leadership instructor at the U.S. Naval Academy, and is a former Naval Flight Officer. Cory led brand and event marketing teams at General Mills, Newell-Rubbermaid, and Johnsonville Sausage. His new book is *The Lens of Leadership: Being the Leader Others WANT to Follow.*

Twitter:
@CoryBouck

LinkedIn:
www.linkedin.com/in/coryabouck

Eric Bruner

Chief Technologist

GP Strategies Corporation

Eric Bruner, GP Strategies' Chief Technologist, has been in the enterprise information management field for 20 years. Eric's roles have ranged from project manager, community of practice leader, Director of R&D, and Director of Corporate Operations. As a project manager, Eric has worked with customers implementing ERP applications and other large scale transformations to integrate learning technologies into the overall initiative with emphasis on workforce readiness and organizational impact.

Currently, Eric is leading GP Strategies' research and development efforts with a concentration in enterprise-wide collaboration, innovation management, and agile learning. Prior to GP, Eric held operations and management positions in the U.S. Navy, Department of Energy, General Electric, RWD Technologies, and ANCILE.

Eric holds a M.S.E. in Engineering Management and a B.S. in Engineering from the U.S. Naval Academy.

Eric has been published in *Chief Learning Officer* magazine, *Talent Management* magazine, ASTD, and GP Strategies' Corporate Blog/Webinar Series. He is a frequent presenter at the *Chief Learning Officer* magazine's Annual Symposium, *Chief Learning Officer* magazine's Breakfast Club, and SAP's Sapphire Now.

Twitter:
@ejbruner

LinkedIn:
www.linkedin.com/in/ejbruner

Michelle Burke

Senior Director, Learning and Communications

KeHE Distributors

Michelle Burke has over 18 years of experience in consulting on organizational effectiveness, change management, and performance improvement. She is currently building the learning function from the ground up at KeHE Distributors. Michelle holds a B.A. in English Education, an M.A. in Curriculum & Instruction, and the CPLP & SPHR designations. Michelle is a frequent speaker at national and international conferences including ASTD's international conference, the Masie Center's Learning conference, and local chapter conferences. She is a former board member of the Central Indiana chapter of ASTD.

Twitter:
@LearningGeek22

LinkedIn:
www.linkedin.com/pub/michelle-burke/4/29/7

Jeff Carpenter
Principal
Caveo Learning

Jeff Carpenter is the founding Principal of Caveo Learning and is a trusted thought partner for the learning and development community. For more than 20 years, Jeff has partnered with Fortune 1000 companies to deliver instructional strategy, performance improvement, and organizational development solutions.

In addition to his professional accomplishments, Jeff has taught Master's-level courses at Roosevelt University on adult learning theory and instructional systems design.

Jeff has earned an M.A. in Training and Development from Roosevelt University and a B.A. in Human Resources from the University of Nebraska.

Twitter:
@CaveoLearning

LinkedIn:
www.linkedin.com/in/jeffrcarpenter

Joan Cooney

Director of Sales Training

Combined Insurance

Joan Cooney is the Director of Sales Education at Combined Insurance, a supplemental insurance company. Joan is a dynamic executive with a successful career of leading enterprise-wide projects, product, and organizational implementations resulting in increased growth and profit. She has a 25+ year track record of translating business objectives into actionable plans, and providing decisive leadership to multi-functional and cross-cultural teams.

Twitter:
@JoanCooney

LinkedIn:
www.linkedin.com/pub/joan-cooney/1/809/589

Laura Coons

Colorado Technical University

CTU Faculty and

Ph.D. Candidate, Colorado State University

Laura Coons, Ph.D. candidate at Colorado State University, has held several positions in training and development, including Director of Faculty Development for Colorado Technical University. In that capacity, she oversaw the hiring and training operations for 800–1,400 online instructors. Her research emphasis in these roles has been on supporting virtual and contingent employees; assessing training needs and implementing meaningful development programs; and improving employee experience with technologies. Prior to coaching and training, she was herself a faculty member, teaching in brick-and-mortar, online, and blended environments.

Laura holds both a B.A. and an M.A. in English. She is pursuing her doctoral degree in Organizational Learning, Performance, and Change. The focal point of her current dissertation work is scenario planning as a strategic tool in organizations. This work evaluates the impact of scenarios on organization members.

LinkedIn:
http://www.linkedin.com/pub/laura-coons/65/884/92b

A.D. Detrick
Learning Measurement Consultant
Intrepid Learning

A.D. Detrick, PMP, is a Learning Measurement Consultant for Intrepid Learning. In the 15 years he has spent in the learning industry, he has extensively researched, trained, and written about assessment, evaluation, and psychometrics. A.D. was an inaugural blogger and bi-weekly contributor for *Training* magazine's "Training Day" blog in 2006, and his article, "Moneyball Lessons: Measurement Isn't Just About the Data," originally appeared on the Intrepid Learning blog. He has designed and implemented measurement strategies for organizations of all sizes, including some of the world's largest corporations.

A.D. earned his Bachelor's degree from Roosevelt University in Chicago.

Twitter:
@IL_AD
LinkedIn:
www.linkedin.com/in/addetrick

Alex Draper

VP North America

ProfitAbility

Alex Draper has more than 10 years of experience in learning and development and currently leads the Americas Operations for ProfitAbility Business Simulations, a global leader in simulation design. He focuses on enhancing leadership development curricula with new and innovative experiential learning solutions that accelerate behavior change. Alex built the Americas operations from scratch, after being sent over from the United Kingdom headquarters seven years ago. He consults, designs, facilitates, and coaches on leadership development programs that use simulations at the core. Alex holds an B.A. (Hons) in Teaching from the University of West of England Bristol, and is a master ProfitAbility facilitator/designer. He is also still a keen rugby player, playing for the Chicago Riot Rugby Club.

Twitter:
@AlexDraperPBS

LinkedIn:
www.linkedin.com/pub/alex-draper/3/11a/694

Wendy Fencl

Global Director, Talent Development
formerly Heidrick & Struggles and
Ph.D. Candidate, Bellevue University

Wendy Fencl, Ph.D. candidate at Bellevue University, was formerly the Global Director of Talent Development for Heidrick & Struggles, providing support for global talent management initiatives and learning. Wendy has over 25 years of experience in the design of change initiatives, performance and reward systems, learning and development strategies, and competency-based staffing and succession processes.

Wendy has been featured in media as diverse as WWJ NewsRadio's Daily Dash and WorkSpan. She has presented in person and via webcast for hr.com, Society for Human Resource Management (SHRM), Human Resource Management Association of Chicago (HRMAC), and ASTD. Wendy presented at the national SHRM conference, and has been a member of HRMAC's Summit Committee and several interest groups' panels.

Wendy has a B.A. in Psychology, Premedical Studies from the University of Notre Dame, and an MBA in Organizational Development and Finance from Northwestern University. She is pursuing her doctoral degree in Human Capital Management.

LinkedIn:
www.linkedin.com/pub/wendy-fencl/3/b59/838

Paulo Goelzer

IGA Coca-Cola Institute

President & CEO

Paulo Goelzer joined IGA in 1994 and focused his attention on international growth, franchise development, and global learning. Today, he is the CEO and President of the IGA Coca-Cola Institute, a corporate university that provides the international retail industry with learning and development programs. The Institute serves more than 6,000 businesses, providing learning strategies, a center for expertise, coaching, and leadership development.

Paulo consulted globally with executives and business owners to design and implement the Institute's state-of-the art development programs. He manages the ongoing production of strategic course curricula, determining budget, selection of vendors, and securing subject matter experts, as well as acting as leadership development facilitator and coach for multiple companies and executives.

Paulo began his career in the food industry very early, working in his family's food business. He was also a Senior Strategy and Consumer Package Goods Industry Consultant for a German/Brazilian consulting company, a researcher and consultant for the Brazilian Wholesaler Association (ABAD), and a marketing director for a CPG company.

He serves as a Distinguished Visiting Scholar for the Ph.D. program in Organization Development at Benedictine University and Springfield College-Illinois. He also serves as a visiting professor at the Graduate School of Business at UNISC in Brazil. He has contributed numerous articles on management, organizational learning, cross cultural marketing, and leadership. He co-authored the textbook, *Distribuição de Classe Mundial* (IMAM), and a chapter in *Advances in Global Leadership* (Elsevier Science).

LinkedIn:
www.linkedin.com/pub/paulo-goelzer-ph-d/5/b41/775

Tom Griffin

Director of Learning, Development & Communications
Sears Holdings Corporation

Tom Griffin is the Director of Learning, Development & Communications at Sears Holdings Corporation for the Information & Technology Group and is responsible for the design and execution of business unit learning, organization development, and communication strategy. In this role, he ensured that associates and leaders at all levels are provided with the training, education, and developmental experiences and resources needed to deliver the ideal customer experience and build a culture of sustainable excellence. Prior to working at Sears, Tom was the VP Organizational Learning & Chief Teaching Officer at U.S. Cellular.

He has extensive experience in the leadership and organization development field, change management, and adult learning methodology. He is a published author, adjunct faculty member for the Chicago School of Professional Psychology, frequent conference speaker, and a winner of the Organization Development Network's 2003 Chicago Impact Award for Organization Development Excellence for large scale Appreciative Inquiry. He is a co-author of *The Appreciative Inquiry Summit: A Practitioner's Guide to Leading Large Group Change* and a contributing author to the *2008 Handbook of Organization Development*, a Sage Publication. His work has also appeared in *Leadership Wired* (Maxwell Leadership Center), *Leadership Excellence, Chief Learning Officer* magazine, and *T+D* magazine.

LinkedIn:
www.linkedin.com/pub/thomas-j-griffin-ph-d/20/945/a0a

Terrence C. Hackett

Senior Manager

Deloitte

Terrence C. Hackett has been a learning professional in multiple capacities for over 20 years. He began his career as a journalist in the Chicago area covering education in the state of Illinois. He moved on from journalism to design and develop award-winning software for elementary and middle schools for a small company in Chicago called Jellyvision. He was part of the design team that created the ground-breaking interactive CD-ROM program, "You Don't Know Jack." In 2001, he joined Deloitte Consulting where he assisted a wide range of corporate clients to optimize their learning strategies in the advent of web-based learning and new, robust learning management systems. From 2003–2008, Terrence operated his own consulting company that specialized in learning and technology. He served Fortune 100 corporations, public and private schools, and other educational organizations. In 2008, he returned to Deloitte to join the Tax Learning and Development team. Today, he specializes in innovation and learning design, and leads the team's efforts around on-demand learning, mobile learning, and testing.

Terrence has a B.A. in Literature from the University of Illinois and an M.A. in Education from Harvard University. Among his publications is his 2001 article for Reading Online called "Making the Student the Star."

LinkedIn:
www.linkedin.com/pub/terry-hackett/0/781/567

Lacey Jennings
Director, Client Management/
Senior Learning Consultant
Intrepid Learning

Lacey Jennings is Director, Client Management for Intrepid Learning, a consulting and learning solutions company. She is an award-winning designer and product developer with more than 20 years of experience in the learning industry. Industry recognition for her efforts includes Human Resource Executive Training, Training Product of the Year 2008; CODiE Finalist, 2008; and Bersin and Associates Learning Leaders, Vendor Innovation, 2009.

Twitter:
@laceycj

LinkedIn:
www.linkedin.com/in/laceycj

Linh Lawler

Manager – Talent & Leadership Strategy

Allstate Insurance Company

Linh Lawler has over 12 years of experience as a leader in talent management and development. She has worked in several industries, including financial and healthcare. She is currently at Allstate Insurance Company as their Leadership Development Lead Consultant with oversight over talent solutions for over 5,000 first-level and mid-level leaders.

LinkedIn:
www.linkedin.com/pub/linh-lawler/9/337/47b

DeBorah Lenchard
Director of Education & Talent Development

Spot Trading

As the Director of Education and Talent Development at Spot Trading since 2008, DeBorah Lenchard develops and leads the organization's learning strategy in order to support the many challenges Spot faces in the highly competitive financial markets. DeBorah designs programs for Spot to grow the knowledge base and technical expertise of over 150 employees from diverse backgrounds working in cross-functional teams. Working individually with employees, DeBorah develops future leaders, supports managers and C-level, and nurtures employees' careers in a collaborative learning environment. Spot is a proprietary trading firm built on applied technology. The company's supportive learning environment has contributed to multiple recognition as one of the "Best and Brightest Companies to Work For™" in Chicago and nationally. Additionally, Spot was named a *Chicago Tribune* Top Workplace in 2013.

Prior to Spot, DeBorah held a variety of organizational learning and development roles, including over 25 years at CME Group, where she created and led the Education Department, focusing on members and customers in a blended education approach as well as CME team/leader development.

DeBorah has a B.A. from Ripon College, an MBA from DePaul University, an M.A. in English Language & English Literature from the University of Chicago, and an M.A.T. in Education from Lewis University.

LinkedIn:
www.linkedin.com/pub/deborah-lenchard/3/b70/266

Laci Loew

Principal Analyst and
Practice Leader Talent Management,
Brandon Hall Group

A principal-level consultant and analyst based in Las Vegas, NV, Laci Loew is expert in all areas of human capital management, particularly leadership, leadership development, and succession management. She has worked in the public and private sectors, consulting global and matrix Fortune companies across all industries on a wide variety of talent initiatives. Some of her more notable accomplishments include the design, development, implementation, and measurement of leadership strategy; leadership development strategy; high-potential strategy; assessments; and the integration of talent processes. Having in-depth industry knowledge—and recognized as a published thought leader and expert—she has refined and improved organizations' differentiation in the market by bringing unique insights, an empirical point of view, thought-provoking ideas, and compelling solution recommendations. She leverages holistic and integrated solutions, builds trusted partnerships, and consults on strategies that generate measurable business impact.

Laci holds a B.S. in Psychology from the University of Illinois at Urbana-Champaign and an MBA from Keller Graduate School of Management, graduating summa cum laude from both institutions. She is currently pursuing her Ph.D. in I/O Psychology at Walden University.

Twitter:
@LaciLoew

LinkedIn:
www.linkedin.com/pub/laci-loew/1/296/bb3

Jenny Massoni

Global Lead, Training Design & Development

Astellas Pharma Global Development Inc.

Jenny Massoni is the Global Lead, Training Design & Development at Global Strategic Operations, Astellas Pharma. She is responsible for the creation and deployment of process, technical, and quality training for individuals supporting drug development. Jenny has 14 years of experience in training and development, and has delivered many speaking engagements at local and national conferences, including Q1 Learning Technologies and Chicago eLearning & Technology Showcase.

LinkedIn:
www.linkedin.com/in/jennymassoni

John R. Mattox, II

Director of Research

KnowledgeAdvisors

John R. Mattox, II, Ph.D., is the Director of Research at KnowledgeAdvisors, a learning analytics company. He is the author of several articles about training evaluation and learning metrics. His works have appeared in *T+D* magazine, *Chief Learning Officer* magazine, and *ELearning!* magazine, among others.

LinkedIn:
www.linkedin.com/pub/john-r-mattox-ii-ph-d/7/84/5b8

Andy Maus

Director, Talent

Claire's Stores Inc.

Andy Maus is currently Director, Talent for Claire's Stores Inc., where he leads the talent acquisition, learning and development, and talent management functions. Prior to Claire's, Andy has held a variety of roles in both Learning and Development and HR in organizations, including U.S. Foods, Discover, and Sears Holdings.

Andy has an MBA from Northwestern University, an M.A. in I/O Psychology and a B.S. in Psychology from Western Michigan University. He currently sits on HRMAC's Leadership Series Committee.

Twitter:
@Andy_Maus

LinkedIn:
www.linkedin.com/pub/andy-maus/3/264/b67

Tom Morehead

Global Managing Director & Lecturer

Crescendo and Kellogg School of Management

Tom Morehead is Global Managing Director of Crescendo, a management consulting firm which helps organizations optimize leadership, teams, and culture. Tom co-authored *Build the Culture Advantage*, a top-rated 2014 business book which provides a strategic approach to building and sustaining high performance organizations. He also partners as faculty-founder on CultureUniversity.com, a global resource dedicated to sharing best practices on business and company culture.

Prior to Crescendo, Tom held leadership positions in a variety of line management and consulting roles with companies including Quaker Oats/Gatorade, Towers Perrin, and Zurich Financial Services. As an alumni of the Kellogg School of Management at Northwestern University, Tom also serves as a Mentor, Executive Coach, and Lecturer. He also provides leadership for NGOs and Non-Profit Boards, including serving as an American Red Cross charity runner for the 2013/2014 Boston Marathon.

Twitter:
@GlobalCoachTom

LinkedIn:
www.linkedin.com/pub/tom-morehead-mba-sphr/7/9aa/980

Heather Muir

Director of Marketing

Mandel Communications

Heather Muir directs Mandel's marketing, branding, and communications strategies, in collaboration with the Executive Team. In addition, Heather leads Mandel's public and industry relations activities. Prior to joining Mandel in 2010, Heather held several marketing and communications roles within the learning and training industry, and is an active member of ASTD; Training Industry, Inc.; eLearningGuild; and the Association of Briefing Program Managers (ABPM).

Heather holds a B.A. from the University of California, Davis, and has completed graduate courses in business and entrepreneurship at the University of Washington.

LinkedIn:
www.linkedin.com/in/heathermuir

Aaron Olson
Chief Talent Officer
Aon

As Global Head of Talent Management, Aaron Olson is responsible for talent and organizational development at Aon. His team manages executive development, performance management, professional development, and succession planning for Aon's 66,000 colleagues around the world.

Aaron has over 20 years of experience consulting with clients and leading initiatives related to talent management, executive succession, and organizational development.

Beyond Aon, Aaron serves as adjunct faculty at Northwestern University, where he teaches graduate courses in talent strategy and leadership development. He is also co-author of the forthcoming book, *Leading with Strategic Thinking* (Wiley 2015).

Twitter:
@aaronkolson
LinkedIn:
www.linkedin.com/in/aaronkolson

Lisa Perez

Human Resources Executive

formerly Accenture and Kohl's Corporation

Lisa Perez is a Human Resources executive with over 18 years of experience in three Fortune 500 companies.

She began her career as a consultant in Accenture's human capital practice. She spent seven years creating and implementing organization effectiveness strategies for Fortune 500 companies, including enterprise-wide customer service systems.

Lisa had P&L responsibility for a biomedical training department at GE Healthcare, where she turned a business from negative profits to over $1M in revenue in a 24-month period. Lisa led a team of 12 learning professionals and operations staff.

Lisa spent nine years at Kohl's Corporation, a $19B retailer. She built and implemented a human capital management infrastructure to support Kohl's rapid growth. Lisa led the OD function for the company, including three teams responsible for learning services, leadership development, and organization effectiveness.

Lisa was a speaker at the Ken Blanchard Companies annual conference, where she presented best practices and ROI analysis for executive coaching programs.

LinkedIn:
www.linkedin.com/pub/lisa-perez/11/642/b01

Pamela S. Puryear, Ph.D.

Vice President, Organization Development

and Chief Talent Officer

Hospira

Pamela S. Puryear, Ph.D., is a business leader, thought leader, and OD practice leader with over 25 years of experience, including 10 years in the real estate investment advisory industry, 12 years as an external Organization Development consultant, and 5 years leading an Organization Development practice in a Fortune 100 company. She has worked and consulted globally and across a number of different industry sectors, including financial services, healthcare, professional services, consumer products, insurance, and education.

Pam's professional passion is performance excellence, and from her diverse professional experiences, she has developed a unique perspective on what creates and sustains excellence. She has worked with individuals, teams, and organizations to excel by assessing needs, and offering solutions that impact performance and productivity. With an MBA and a Ph.D., she considers financial and human factors, and how to manage both using sound organizational management thinking and focused business metrics.

In 2014, Pam was profiled and appeared on the cover of the February issue of *Chief Learning Officer* magazine. She was honored to be selected as an award winner in the Business Impact category for the 2014 Learning in Practice awards, sponsored by *Chief Learning Officer* magazine. In 2012, Pam was the recipient of the 2012 Rising Star Award by *Human Resource Executive* magazine. Pam is a frequent speaker at human capital conferences.

Through LinkedIn and her website JoinDrPam.com, Pam seeks to develop a virtual community of practice to keep current on how individuals, teams, and enterprises work, thrive, and drive toward excellence.

Pam holds a Ph.D. in Organizational Psychology, an MBA from Harvard Business School, and a B.A. in Psychology with a concentration in Organizational Behavior from Yale University.

LinkedIn:
https://www.linkedin.com/in/joindrpam

Carmela Richeson
Manager, Learning and Development
Claire's Stores Inc.

Carmela Richeson has a passion for developing talent that started by teaching people how to use their copy machines! From the ins and outs of copiers and networking technical training delivery, to developing strategic L&D programs to increase internal promotion rates in retail leadership, the story unfolds.

Carmela's key achievements in the retail space have been focused on development and execution of strategic on-boarding, high potential leadership, and overall talent development programs as well as being a key partner in talent management and organizational effectiveness efforts.

Twitter:
@Melriche

LinkedIn:
www.linkedin.com/pub/carmela-richeson/11/b25/617

Marty Rosenheck

CEO, Chief Learning Strategist

Cognitive Advisors

Marty Rosenheck, Ph.D., is CEO, Chief Learning Strategist at Cognitive Advisors, makers of the TREK Learning Experience Manager—mobile software that optimizes the development of workplace skills by managing and tracking on-the-job learning, and enabling nano-coaching.

He is a thought leader and sought-after consultant, speaker, and writer on the application of cognitive science research to learning and performance. He has been helping people and organizations develop expert performance for over 30 years. Marty has designed award-winning learning and performance support systems, conducted needs assessments, developed curricula, applied knowledge harvesting techniques, created virtual learning environments, and developed social learning strategies for many nonprofit and for-profit organizations. He has shared his ideas on learning and technology in numerous presentations and workshops. His writing has appeared in *T+D* magazine, *Chief Learning Officer* magazine, and many other publications. He most recently led a team that won the ASTD Excellence in Practice award.

Twitter:
@mbr1online

LinkedIn:
www.linkedin.com/in/martyrosenheck

Babak Salimi

Sr. Director Product Marketing –
Talent Mgmt & Mobile Solutions
Saba

Babak Salimi is Sr. Director at Saba, responsible for marketing Saba's Intelligent Talent Management platform. Babak has 20 years of industry experience with talent management, workforce planning, social learning, mobile collaboration, IT, security, and compliance solutions.

Prior to Saba, Babak drove marketing, business development, and product strategy for market leading organizations such as Agiliance, Workshare, GreenBorder (acquired by Google), Sygate (acquired by Symantec), Nortel, and IBM.

Babak holds an M.S. in Technology Management and a B.S. in Engineering with honors from McGill University.

Twitter:
@babaksalimi

LinkedIn:
www.linkedin.com/in/babaksalimi

Lisa Schumacher
Director of Education Strategies
McDonald's Corporation

Lisa Schumacher is the Director of Education Strategies at McDonald's Corporation. She has more than 10 years of experience in organizational learning and development. Lisa currently is responsible for leading the development and execution of education solutions to enhance workforce capability, and the employee talent pipeline for McDonald's.

In her previous role at the Council for Adult and Experiential Learning (CAEL) as the Director of WorkforceChicago, Lisa collaborated with Chicago area CEOs, managing a business-led initiative that identified and disseminated best-practice learning strategies and policies. Prior to that, Lisa was the Director of the University of Chicago Medical Center's Academy, where she provided leadership in developing the organization's overall learning strategy.

Lisa completed her B.A. and M.A. in Communication at Purdue University.

LinkedIn:
www.linkedin.com/pub/lisa-hunt-schumacher/8/6b0/624

B.K. Simerson, Ed.D.

Faculty – School of Education and Social Policy

Northwestern University

B. Keith (B.K.) Simerson, Ed.D., provides consultation and executive coaching to professional services firms; colleges and universities; all branches of the U.S. military, foreign and U.S. government agencies; and clients across 19 industries. He is the author of books on strategy formulation and execution, leadership, career planning and transitions, and executive development program evaluation. B.K. is co-author of the forthcoming book, *Leading with Strategic Thinking* (Wiley 2015). In addition to consulting, he serves as adjunct faculty at Northwestern University, where he teaches graduate courses in leadership and strategy.

B.K. earned his Ed.D. with an emphasis in Management and Organizational Development from the University of North Carolina at Greensboro.

LinkedIn:
www.linkedin.com/pub/bk-simerson-ed-d/2/376/427

Bill Terpstra

Operations Director, Learning Organization

Motorola Solutions

Bill Terpstra is the operations director of learning for Motorola Solutions. His team is responsible for delivering the most effective learner experience, thus maximizing the impact of learning. In addition to the management and improvement of learning systems, software, and tools, his team also leads various centers of learning best practices, including certification, technology innovation, strategy, and communications.

Bill started his career in engineering. He joined Motorola in 1994 and has led global teams in system integration, program management, technical documentation, and training design and development.

Bill holds a B.S. in Electrical Engineering from the University of Illinois, an MBA from IIT Stuart School of Business, and a master's certificate in Program Management from the George Washington University. He is also a certified Program Management Professional from the Program Management Institute.

LinkedIn:
www.linkedin.com/in/billterpstra

Judy Whitcomb, SPHR

Vice President, Human Resources,

Learning & Organizational Development

Vi

Judy Whitcomb has more than 25 years of experience in various human resources roles, including 19 years with United Airlines. Currently, as Vice President of Human Resources, Learning & Organizational Development, Judy leads Vi's human resources strategy, including compensation and benefits, learning and organizational development, recruitment, and payroll. Vi is a national luxury senior living provider.

Since joining Vi, Judy has led the learning, and organizational development and effectiveness efforts for the company. This has culminated in an array of acknowledgments, including being selected by *Chief Learning Officer* magazine as Best Small Company for Learning in 2012 and 2013; being distinguished as *Chief Learning Officer* magazine's LearningElite; *Training* magazine's Top 125; and *E-Learning!* magazine's Top 100 Learning Organizations for the last three consecutive years.

She earned a bachelor's degree from DePaul University, an MBA from Roosevelt University, and is SPHR certified. Judy is a frequent speaker at national and international conferences, including *Chief Learning Officer* magazine's annual symposiums, and is a contributor to professional publications, including *Training* magazine.

Twitter:
@WhitJudy

LinkedIn:
www.linkedin.com/pub/judy-whitcomb/4/a77/767

Ann Wyatt

Regional Vice President

HealthFitness

Ann Wyatt is a Regional Vice President in Account Management at HealthFitness, an award-winning, URAC- and NCQA-accredited provider of health management, corporate fitness, and condition management solutions. In her role, she oversees the startup of new health management and corporate fitness programs; the transition of existing programs; employee recruiting and training; program quality assurance; and operations management. Ann brings 25 years of experience with employee health programs.

Twitter:
@hfit

LinkedIn:
www.linkedin.com/pub/ann-wyatt/1/b76/917

Tiffany Yates

Doctoral Department Chair
Colorado Technical University

Dr. Tiffany Yates is the current Doctoral Department Chair with Colorado Technical University. In this administrative position, she leads approximately 100 faculty members. Her team is responsible for the learning process of 500 doctorate students in a variety of concentration areas focusing on computer science and management. She values the vital scholar-practitioner model by enabling student engagement around career progression. Her research efforts are in organization development, employee engagement, strategic organization design, innovation, and large-scale change initiatives. Dr. Yates is published within the Academy of Management, Midwest Academy of Management, Southwest Academy of Management, ISEOR Division of the Academy of Management, American Society for Quality, and the Organization Development Journal.

Dr. Yates holds an M.A. in Economics and B.B.A. in Marketing. She was also awarded a Ph.D. from Benedictine University in Organization Development. Her dissertation is entitled, "Developing a Culture for Continuous Innovation: A Qualitative Study of Organization Development." Her dissertation research examines how dimensions of organizational culture affect continuous innovation.

Twitter:
@YatesTiffany

LinkedIn:
www.linkedin.com/pub/tiffany-yates-ph-d/16/2b1/914/

Gabi Zolla

Chief Operating Officer
Council for Adult and Experiential Learning

Gabi Zolla currently serves as Chief Operating Officer at CAEL, the Council for Adult and Experiential Learning. She oversees finance, human resources, marketing, and grants management, while also leading CAEL's Innovation and Policy Unit. Gabi joined CAEL in July 2000 as the Director of the President's Office, before moving into the position of VP for Research, Policy, and Programs. Before joining CAEL, Gabi was the Communications Manager for the American Bar Association's Commission on Women. She has an extensive background in philanthropy, having worked at both the Ford Foundation and the Annie E. Casey Foundation.

Gabi holds a B.A. in English from Knox College and a J.D. from New York University School of Law.

Twitter:
@CAELnews

LinkedIn:
www.linkedin.com/pub/gabi-zolla/10/946/367

⌘ ACKNOWLEDGMENTS ⌘

The Executive Learning Exchange is a consortium of senior learning leaders from Chicagoland, Central Illinois, Central Indiana, Milwaukee, and Twin Cities who are committed to promoting greater visibility, influence, and professional opportunities among its members. We focus on business results, plain and simple. We attract the best and brightest. We delight in the ability to connect with our peers from companies such as Abbott, AbbVie, Accenture, Allstate, Aon, Astellas, Baker Tilly, Baxter, Bellevue University, Bison Gear, Brandon Hall Group, Bersin by Deloitte, BlueCross BlueShield of IL, BMO Harris Bank, Brunswick, CAEL, Caliper, Caveo, Deloitte, CIGNA, Collegis Education, Colorado Technical University, Combined Insurance, Discover, Froedtert & Community Health, Grant Thornton, Harley-Davidson, IGA Coca-Cola Institute, Intrepid Learning, Institute for Corporate Productivity, Johnson Controls, KeHE Distributors, Kraft Foods, Lurie Children's, McDonald's Corporation, Motorola Solutions, Stepan, Sysmex, University of Phoenix, Walgreens, and many more to gain valuable insights on what's working, what's not, and what's ahead.

This collaborative book could not have become a reality without the amazing support from our powerful network of learning and talent development leaders. We would like to acknowledge specifically the members of Executive Learning Exchange's CLO/CTO Group. Their advice steers our initiatives as we continue to expand our capabilities. At the time of this writing, those leaders include: Gail Leiber, Abbott; Angela Lane, AbbVie; Samir Desai, Accenture; Steve King, Allstate; Aaron Olson, Aon; Anne Allison, Astellas; Tim Kirkpatrick, Baxter; Mary Jo Burfeind, Healthcare Service Corporation (BCBS-IL); Marie Reynolds, BMO Harris Bank; Karen Kocher, CIGNA; Jane Dowd, College of American Pathologists; Tim Taylor, Combined Insurance; Kim Witt, Discover; Richard Rykhus, Grant Thornton; Paulo Goelzer, IGA Coca-Cola Institute; Michelle Burke, KeHE Distributors; Diana Thomas, McDonald's Corporation; Joe Misurac, Stepan; Sal Venegas, Walgreens; Alysa Parks, ZS.

Lastly, there are many former CLO/CTO Group members who have moved on, and, even though they no longer attend our quarterly meetings, many of them stay active by providing their thought leadership to assist with the building of our next generation of learning leaders. One of these former CLO/CTO Group members, Corinne Miller, contributed significant effort to ensure that clear communication was used for the lessons learned in this book.

Executive Learning
EXCHANGE
Leading Learning Innovations of the Future

THERE'S NEVER A LAST WORD AMONG OUR GROUP.

The experienced words in this book are just a small snapshot of what the most powerful network of learning leaders has to offer. What's so powerful? We focus on business results, plain and simple. We attract the best and brightest. Imagine knowing and being able to connect with your peers from companies such as the thought leaders who contributed their lessons learned to this book. Gaining valuable insights on what's working, what's not, and what's ahead provides a continuous stream of learning that fuels continuous business results.

For inquiries regarding citations in this book, please contact the contributor(s) of the essay. Engage your learning and talent development professionals with the Executive Learning Exchange's thought leaders by sharing our YouTube channel and attending our in-person events. If you are interested in reading any of the research cited in this book, please contact the contributor of the essay.

YouTube:
www.youtube.com/learningexecutive

Upcoming Learning Leaders' Events:
www.LearningExecutive.com

If you have questions, please email info@learningexecutive.com.

Twitter:
@LearningLeader

LinkedIn:
www.linkedin.com/in/learningexecutive

Made in the USA
Charleston, SC
06 September 2014